SIR ALEX FERGUSON
FIFTY DEFINING FIXTURES

SIR ALEX FERGUSON

FERGUSON

FIFTY DEFINING FIXTURES

Iain McCartney

AMBERLEY

First published 2013

Amberley Publishing
The Hill, Stroud
Gloucestershire, GL5 4EP

www.amberley-books.com

British Library Cataloguing in Publication Data.
A catalogue record for this book is available from the British Library.

ISBN 978 1 4456 2147 0 (print)
ISBN 978 1 4456 2153 1 (ebook)

Typeset in 9.5pt on 13pt Sabon.
Typesetting and Origination by Amberley Publishing.
Printed in the UK.

Contents

Introduction

Alex Ferguson. Over 1,500 competitive games as manager of Manchester United Football Club, present at all but a mere handful of them, with countless friendly fixtures taking that total soaring even higher. Throw into the mix another 536 as manager of Aberdeen and ten with Scotland, along with however many there were with St Mirren and East Stirlingshire, plus over 300 outings as a player with Queens Park, St Johnstone, Dunfermline, Rangers, Falkirk, Ayr United and Scotland, and you are hitting well over 2,500 games. Some career!

Indeed, it was some career. A white-knuckle roller-coaster ride from the grass roots of Scottish football (I haven't even bothered to include his appearances with the famed Drumchapel Amateurs) to the world stage: a career of cups and controversy; history and histrionics. A career, certainly as a manager, unmatched in the modern game and arguably unmatched in the history of football, full stop.

This book is not just another biographical tome looking back at the life of Sir Alexander Chapman Ferguson CBE. Perhaps in a way it is, but it does so in a completely different fashion than any of the others, taking you, the reader, over a period of some fifty-five years, looking at the games that helped shape, and later define, the footballing career of a true legend.

Author's Note

While reading through this book, some of you, perhaps all of you, will ask why this particular match was not included or why that particular match was included.

Selecting the fifty games for this book was even more difficult than writing it.

Some obviously picked themselves, while others I felt were worthy of their place. I could probably have selected two or three more from his final season.

But at the end of the day, the number was fifty and the pages that follow reveal those chosen.

1

Stranraer *v.* Queens Park

15 November 1958

Alex Ferguson had joined Drumchapel Amateurs from the Harmony Row Boys' Club as a fourteen-year-old in September 1956, spending two years with the club famed for its production line of players who were to progress to the professional game. Two years later, he was on the move, not to the professional ranks, but to another noted amateur side, Queens Park. The 'Spiders', although amateurs, played in the Scottish Second Division and it was here at the age of sixteen that he took his first tentative steps in the senior game.

Stranraer: Travers, Mason, McLean, King (1 pen.), Simpson, McKnight, Small, R. McKechnie, Phillips, Moore (1), Imrie.
Queens Park: W. C. Pinkerton, W. McBride, W. Hastie, R. Cromar, R. McKinvin, W. Bell, W. Omand, A. Ferguson (1), C. Church, R. Wood, M. Darroch.
Score: 2-1
Attendance: 1,650

'Queens Park debut day. Two inside-forwards, Alec (*sic*) Ferguson and Robbie Wood played their first game at Stranraer today,' proclaimed the *Glasgow Evening Times* of Saturday 15 November. 'Ferguson is a youngster who began his football adventures with the Queens Park youth team this season and has made such rapid progress that he just had to be given his big chance today.'

A big chance it certainly was, as the previous Saturday young master Ferguson could have been found playing in the Scottish Amateur Cup second-round replay for a 'Queens Park Hampden XI' at Eaglesham. Although putting his side 2-1 in front, he could not prevent a cup exit with a 4-3 defeat after extra time.

On the morning of 15 November, he left the south side of Glasgow with his teammates, heading for one of the outposts of the Scottish game – Stranraer, better known for its ferry terminal than its football team.

There was certainly no fanfare of trumpets that afternoon in south-west Scotland, nor were there any Queens Park pen pictures in the somewhat spartan four-page match programme to inform the meagre gathering at Stair Park as to who the dark-haired, boyish-looking 'Ferguson' was at No. 8.

The game, described in two local papers as 'a dour struggle from start to finish', saw the home side begin well, with Imrie coming close in the opening stages, but their attacks were frequently stopped by any means possible, as whenever a Stranraer player went to get past them, if he was at arm's length, then he was brought down unceremoniously by a Queens Park defender.

A Cromar effort was saved by Travers, but with both sides seemingly content simply to prevent the other from scoring, the first half drew to a close, having failed to produce anything in the way of goals.

If boring could be used to describe that opening forty-five minutes, then the second half was anything but, sparkling into life immediately after the restart when King, the Stranraer right-half, missed a through ball and Ferguson was on it in a flash. Finding himself clean through on goal, there was a slight hesitation as Travers moved out from his line and, as the teenager shot for goal, the 'keeper blocked the shot with his body before diving on it as Church moved in.

Queens Park were enjoying their best period of the game and both Ferguson and Wood tested Travers with fine shots, but it was at the opposite end that the opening goal materialised in the fifty-seventh minute. Small forced a corner on the right and from his flag kick, with three Stranraer forwards left unmarked, Moore headed home.

Within five minutes, all hell broke loose.

Simpson of Stranraer and Church of Queen Park clashed in midfield and fell to the ground. The latter appeared to be holding his opponent's legs, while Simpson had his elbow in the face of the Queens Park man. A kicking match soon developed and Cromar and McKnight rushed in to separate the pair, but found it impossible as the vendetta continued, leaving the referee with little option but to send both players off.

With both guilty individuals barely down the tunnel, Stranraer increased their lead, centre-half McKinvin handling the ball inside the area and King making no mistake from the spot. After this, Stranraer upped the pace and Pinkerton had to save well from Imrie to prevent a third, while the same player should have done better soon afterwards when clean through on goal.

Slowly, Queens Park began to ease their way back into the game, forgetting their underhand tactics for the time being, and managed to pull a goal back. The goal has always been credited to the sixteen-year-old debutant 'Alec Ferguson', but in the *Galloway Advertiser and Wigtonshire Free Press* for 20 November, the goal is described as follows: 'Darroch (the Queens Park outside left) raced down the left wing, beating three men and flashing a brilliant shot past Travers. It was a really worthwhile goal and put Queens Park on their mettle.'

From the *Galloway Gazette* of 22 November, however, young master Ferguson is indeed credited with the goal: 'Stranraer were doing all the running, but surprisingly enough Queens reduced the leeway when Ferguson, not yet seventeen, nipped in and gave Travers no chance.'

Sadly, there was little time left for the youngster to complete his memorable debut with an equaliser, but no matter; it was the start of what was to be an exceptional career, despite his initial appearance being in a such a robust fixture, full of fierce tackling and deplorable tactics, with both teams described in the *Gazette* as 'not caring less who won the game'.

In his autobiography, *Managing My Life*, the debutant wrote, 'That debut confrontation with Stranraer was closer to nightmare. My troubles began with the decision to play me at outside-right [although he was listed as inside-right in the programme and the press], which didn't suit me at all – nor did their left-back, a little tank by the name of McKnight. After a collision had put the two of us on the ground, the bastard bit me. At half-time, the official in charge of our team, Jackie Gardiner, roasted me for not being competitive enough.' When the youngster complained that he had been bitten, he was simply told to bite him back.

Welcome to the world of professional football.

2

Rangers *v.* St Johnstone

21 December 1963

Alex Ferguson left the south side of Glasgow and Hampden Park on 11 June 1960, signing for St Johnstone while still retaining his amateur status. Although a step up the ladder, there were still countless rungs to be encountered before anything like the top could be reached.

At times, it must have actually have felt like a step backwards, as first-team football, something that he had often been denied with Queens Park, was not something that he was guaranteed.

Indeed, with 1963 edging towards 1964, he was in a determined mood to leave the Perth club for pastures new, with Raith Rovers showing considerable interest in signing him back in October.

Despite the lack of first-team opportunities around this time, Alex Ferguson remained loyal to his club and gave 100 per cent in every game, a trait that he expected from his players many years later when he hung up his boots and took over the role of manager.

Rangers: Ritchie, Shearer, Provan (1 pen.), Grieg, McKinnon, Wood, Henderson, McMillan, Millar, McLean, Brand (1).
St Johnstone: Fallon, McFadyen, Richmond, Townsend, McIntyre, McCarry, Flannagan, Craig, McIntyre, Ferguson (3), Kemp.
Score: 3-2
Attendance: 15,000 or 12,000 (depending on which newspaper you go by)

Brought up a five-minute walk from Ibrox, the home of Glasgow Rangers, a stadium he used to sneak into as a boy, and where he collected the empty beer bottles from the terraces at full-time and took them to the nearest shop to claim the refundable pennies that supplemented his pocket money, Ferguson found himself called upon to play on the turf that he had viewed many times from the steep slopes surrounding the running track, as St Johnstone were in the midst of an injury crisis.

Having been turning out in the unfamiliar half-back position in the Perth reserve side, he was called upon to fill the No. 10 shirt against the Scottish First Division league leaders as something of a last-minute replacement, as his name featured neither in the St Johnstone pen pictures nor the actual team line-ups within the Rangers match programme.

On the Football Pools coupon, it was a dead cert 'home win'. The local boy, however, was to destroy all hopes of securing a fortune for the punters that weekend.

Playing conditions were poor, with the pitch bone-hard due to severe overnight frost, but the promising start by the home side quickly warmed up their support.

With seven minutes gone, Greig fired a 25-yard drive narrowly over, then McMillan, at the heart of every Rangers move, released McLean on a few times, but on each occasion he was to have his efforts blocked by a St Johnstone defender.

In the early exchanges, the visitors seldom troubled Ritchie in the home goal, while at the opposite end Fallon wasn't exactly overworked as, despite holding top spot, Rangers had been booed off the pitch following their previous home game.

McMillan picked out Henderson with yet another accurate pass, but the diminutive winger could only hit the side netting. Millar then got the better of two St Johnstone defenders, but wasted the opportunity by shooting wide of the goal. It was, however, only a matter of time before Rangers scored, and the opening goal finally came nine minutes before the interval, when McMillan released Brand, who placed the ball between Fallon's legs to give the home side the lead.

The second half opened in almost identical fashion to the first, with a Rangers effort flying narrowly over (McLean the culprit on this occasion). But it wasn't all Rangers, Shearer having to clear a Flannagan effort off the line as the visitors began to press. Their persistence paid off in the fifty-third minute when they drew level. Two efforts had been blocked before the ball rebounded off Rangers full-back Shearer, allowing Alex Ferguson to pounce and drive the ball past the left hand of Ritchie in the Rangers goal.

From the restart, Henderson was somewhat unceremoniously brought down by McCarry, then Brand and Townsend got involved in a tussle as the game began to simmer away. Then Ferguson almost notched his second from an identical position to that of his first, but his left-footed effort went just over.

Much to the annoyance of the Rangers support, St Johnstone took the lead on the hour when Ritchie failed to hold a shot from Kemp, and once again Ferguson was on hand to snatch the rebound to score.

In the seventy-second minute, Rangers drew level from the penalty spot after the referee adjudged Townsend to have handled inside the area. The St Johnstone No. 4 was adamant that the ball had hit him on the chest as he threw himself forward, but his protests were to no avail and Provan scored from the spot.

Four minutes later, the visitors were back in front. McIntyre intercepted an attempted back pass by Shearer before pushing the ball into the path for Ferguson who, having been challenged by Greig, lost his footing but still managed to guide the ball over the line.

Five minutes later, he almost made it 4-2, but the headlines for the Saturday night and Sunday newspapers were already written: 'The man who shocked Rangers' in the *Sunday Mail*, 'Alex (He's For Transfer) Busts League Wide Open' in the *Sunday Post* and 'Unhappy Hero. Ferguson – I Still Want to Move' proclaimed by the *Daily Record*.

Despite his hat-trick, the twenty-one-year-old man of the moment insisted after the match that he still wanted to leave St Johnstone.

'I'm only a part-time player, as I work as a tool setter in Glasgow,' said the youngster. 'This means I can't get up to Perth to train, so I just work out on my own at Cathkin [home of the now defunct Third Lanark]. The only time I'm in touch with Saints is a Saturday.'

Leaving Ibrox after the game, unrecognised by the waiting autograph hunters, he was stopped by a reporter and asked about the game, and said, 'I found it difficult to get into the game at first, but I felt a lot better after that first goal. I felt even better when I got the second and really felt on top of the world when I completed my hat-trick.'

His manager, Bobby Brown, was even quicker off the mark than his new star striker, telling the press that 'since Alex Ferguson decided not to go to Raith Rovers we have changed our minds about accepting offers for him – in the meantime at least'.

The future of the promising young striker looked bright.

3

Aberdeen *v.* Real Madrid

11 May 1983

Having eventually left St Johnstone for Dunfermline in 1964, Alex Ferguson continued his rise up the football ladder with Scottish representative honours at both full and Scottish League level, scoring ten goals in seven games with the former, before joining Rangers in 1967. Further Scottish League honours came his way before he moved to Falkirk, seeing out his playing career with Ayr United.

Having taken his coaching badges, the next step was obviously at managerial level and he was more than happy to begin at the bottom, taking up his first such post with East Stirlingshire in July 1964. His stay there was brief to say the least, as he left to join St Mirren the following October.

He took the Paisley club to the First Division championship in 1977/78 and, with his ability and determination beginning to be noticed within the game, it came as no surprise when the opportunity arose to move to a higher level again as Aberdeen came calling in 1978.

It took him a couple of years to find his feet in the north-east and get the club organised to his expected standards. The time taken and the patience shown by the Aberdeen directors paid off and before long they were nudging their way into the Rangers and Celtic domination over the trophies in the Scottish game.

Alex Ferguson's Aberdeen did not simply trample on the fingers of Glasgow, and Scotland's 'big two'; he was to leave them bloodied and bruised, with silver polish very much back on the shopping list at Pittodrie.

Domestic success soon became expected of Aberdeen on a regular basis, but their manager always kept his sights upwards and enjoyed the challenge of European football. Alex Ferguson had his first taste of competitive European football in the 1978/79 season, gaining a back-door entry as Scottish Cup runners-up to Rangers, who had qualified for the European Cup as League champions, but they were to be knocked out as early as the second round by Fortuna Dusseldorf. The following season, this time in the UEFA Cup, they again failed to overcome German opposition – this time it was Eintracht Frankfurt.

The European Cup first came onto Alex Ferguson's radar as a manager in 1980/81, but after defeating Austria Memphis in the opening round, they were paired with an experienced Liverpool side. Having enjoyed a 1-0 victory at Pittodrie, they met their match on Merseyside, losing 4-0. The 1981/82 UEFA Cup competition once again saw Ferguson's team lose to German opposition, with Hamburg knocking them out in the third round.

There was a hint of impatience about the progress being made on the European front, but the Aberdeen manager was filing away each experience, knowing that the opportunity to improve and indeed prove himself would eventually materialise.

Real Madrid: Agustin, Juan José, Metgod, Bonet, Camacho, Angel, Gallego, Stielike, Isidro, Juanito (1 pen.), Santillana. Substitutes: Isidoro San José for Camacho, Salguero for Isidro. Miguel Angel, Gracia and Hernandez not used.
Aberdeen: Leighton, Rougvie, Miller, McLeish, McMaster, Cooper, Strachan, Simpson, Black (1), McGhee, Weir. Substitutes: Hewitt (1) for Black. Gunn, Watson, Kennedy and Angus not used.
Score: 2-1
Attendance: 17,804

Having won the Scottish Cup in 1982, the European Cup Winners' Cup was added to the Aberdeen fixture list for season 1982/83, and their preliminary-round tie against FC Sion was the ideal launching pad for yet another tilt at European football, with the Swiss side demoralised in an 11-1 aggregate win.

If those opponents were obscure, the Albanians of Dinamo Tirana were equally so, although they caused numerous problems for Ferguson's team, who lost out by one solitary goal. It was an even lesser-known opponent in round three, in the shape of Lech Poznan of Poland. Did Alex Ferguson know someone at UEFA?

The Poles were defeated 3-0 as Aberdeen progressed into the quarter-finals. Here, the opposition became much tougher, with the huge spectre of German football once again casting a shadow over Pittodrie as the draw paired Aberdeen with Bayern Munich.

Drawn away in the first leg, Ferguson went for an ultra-cautious defensive display and returned home with a creditable 0-0 draw. The return leg, however, was a potential pitfall, with the Germans twice taking the lead, only for fightbacks that would, in the future, be commonplace with Ferguson teams, as his team stormed into the semi-finals with a 3-2 victory.

It was back to the unfamiliar in the last four, with Waterschei of Belgium the opposition and, having seen off Bayern Munich, there was no way that Aberdeen were going to lose this particular game. But lose in Belgian in the second leg they did, by 1-0; however, having hammered Waterschei 5-1 at home, they were safely through to the final.

There were no Germans waiting to pounce in the final, but there was the formidable name of Real Madrid, under the guidance of former legend Di Stéfano, although the Aberdeen manager was quick to point out, 'We are dealing with the present Real players, not the side which last won in Europe seventeen years ago.

'Our best performance was at Munich against Bayern. If we can repeat that display, we must have a good chance.' He dismissed the current quality to be seen in Spanish football.

'I've seen Real Madrid. There is not much between them and Bayern, although I rate the Germans ahead of them.'

Speaking on the eve of the final, he added, 'There is no sign of excitement, although this will come. No doubt I'll be reaching for the valium nearer the time.'

With the manager having predicted that there would be no nerves shown by his players, Aberdeen, true to his word, settled quickly and could have taken the lead through Simpson as early as the second minute, when the midfielder raced through the middle before shooting narrowly wide. A minute later, Agustin made a hash of a clearance and Strachan snatched the ball, crossing towards Black, but his volley smacked against the Madrid crossbar with the 'keeper well beaten.

But the Aberdeen support had to wait only seven minutes before their favourites took the lead on what was a slippy, greasy playing surface. A Strachan corner was met by the head of McLeish, and the powerful effort cannoned off the body of a Madrid defender, falling nicely for Black to flick home from close range.

Their lead, however, was relatively short-lived, as in the fourteenth minute, McLeish diced with danger, attempting a back pass on the rain-soaked turf. The ball slowed, allowing Santillana to latch onto it. Leighton raced from his goal and, with little in the way of options available to him, brought the Madrid captain down as he attempted to go round the Aberdeen 'keeper. From the resulting spot-kick, Juanito made no mistake.

Having lost such a careless goal, the Aberdeen heads went down, allowing the Spaniards to come more into the game, dominating midfield, with Stielike virtually running the show. Their play at times bordered on the cynical, but they could not, however, convert their superiority into goals, much to the relief of the Aberdeen contingent.

They managed to keep the score at 1-1 until the interval allowed Alex Ferguson the opportunity to galvanise his troops during the half-time break, and as the second half got underway there was a notable difference in Aberdeen's play, with McMaster, Rougvie, Strachan and Weir all coming to the fore. Seven minutes into the second half, a Weir cross was met by Strachan, but his first-time effort bounced off the 'keeper's legs. Agustin also had to do well to keep an effort from Rougvie.

Leighton was called into the action to deal with a long-range effort from Santillana, while a Black header went close. Strachan then beat Metgod, but chipped the ball over the bar when it looked easier to score. Poor finishing at either end failed to produce any further goals during the ninety minutes, and the game drifted into extra time, a half-hour period seemingly better suited to the Scots.

Cooper and Hewitt were both sent crashing to the ground inside the Madrid penalty area, but as the Aberdeen players and supporters shouted for penalties, the referee simply waved play on.

As the minutes slowly ticked away, Madrid showing clear signs of fatigue while the referee continued his inconsistency, it began to look as though the match would be decided on penalties. Leighton was forced into making a superb save from Santillana, while Hewitt, McGhee and Simpson all had opportunities to give Aberdeen the lead as Madrid began to disintegrate.

Then, with eight minutes remaining, Aberdeen broke forward. Weir floated the ball over the heads of two Madrid defenders into the path of McGhee down the left.

Striding past one defender, he crossed into the Madrid penalty area, where Hewitt, on as a substitute for Eric Black in the eighty-seventh minute, stole in marginally in front of Bonet to head home.

Rather ironically, it was Hewitt who had scored the winner against Bayern Munich in the quarter-final, with only eight minutes remaining.

Such was the tiredness of the Madrid players, there was no way that they would come back, and all that the Aberdeen players had to do was ensure that the closing minutes were played out cautiously and risk free.

'We slaughtered them,' proclaimed a jubilant Alex Ferguson. 'The best thing for us was the half-time interval. We lost our way a bit when Juanito got the equaliser.

'But afterwards my only concern was the game staying at 1-1 in extra time and going to penalties to decide the outcome. Real Madrid looked as though they would have been happy with that situation. However, we wanted to settle the game and John Hewitt certainly did that in great style. It sounds corny, but it's a dream come true for all of us at Pittodrie. I had no doubt that we could beat Real.'

4

Oxford United (A)

8 November 1986

Results in the early days of the 1986/87 season had been poor, with only two victories and a draw in the opening eight fixtures, and the 1-0 home defeat by Chelsea leaving Ron Atkinson's team second bottom of the First Division, level on points with Aston Villa, who propped the table up due to having conceded more goals.

Two victories and three draws in the following five games lifted the black cloud hovering over Old Trafford, if only momentarily, but Ron Atkinson was living on borrowed time, with a training ground punch-up between Remi Moses and Jesper Olsen, leaving the Danish winger requiring eleven stiches for a cut above his eye, doing little for team morale.

A 0-0 home draw against Southampton in the Littlewoods Cup, a team United had beaten 5-1 at the same venue only a matter of weeks previously, was sandwiched in between the 1-1 draws against Manchester City and Coventry City, with the replay at the Dell exposing everything that was wrong with the troubled club as they sank to a 4-1 defeat.

Hours later, the national press proclaimed an 'Old Trafford Crisis', with John Sadler writing in The Sun that the next two fixtures were 'Two Games Ron Must Win', while Bob Russell in the Mirror was rather more forthright and got straight to the point under the heading 'Why Ron Must Go'.

Russell, who had reported on United for fifteen years, wrote that, 'It would be in his (Atkinson's) own interest and more importantly, for the sake of the great name of Manchester United and its survival as a First Division giant.' The ink was barely dry on both articles when the news broke that Atkinson had indeed been sacked by United, with chairman Martin Edwards saying that he had been dismissed 'in the light of the team's performance over the last twelve months'.

Terry Venables was an early frontrunner for the vacant manager's chair, but the position had already been filled by the time the Manchester Evening News had hinted that the Barcelona manager was a strong candidate, with Aberdeen's Alex Ferguson having been sounded out, interviewed and appointed. This was a manager who that same Evening News article had mentioned as being more than happy on the east coast of Scotland, and one whose yearly earnings, in excess of £100,000, would be enough to put United off.

It has long been debated that Ferguson had been sounded out prior to Atkinson's sacking, but certainly within an hour of the United board's decision, Aberdeen *chairman Dick Donald's permission had been sought in order to officially speak to the forty-four-year-old Ferguson, and in next to no time he was installed as manager of Manchester United.*

'It is a marvellous feeling,' he declared. 'It is the only job which would ever have me think about quitting Aberdeen.

'Other clubs have made their approaches to me before, but Aberdeen compared favourably with any of them.

'However, United are special. They would attract any manager from anywhere in the world.

'My aim is to make this club the biggest and best in Europe.

'To win in Scotland, I had to break the Old Firm's stranglehold. The situation is similar here. Liverpool and Everton have dominated. Nottingham Forest are currently top, but they will find it a strain to remain there.'

Continuing, he made no attempt to hide his number one aim: 'Winning the League, which hasn't happened at Old Trafford since 1967, is the greatest challenge facing everyone. That is the hurdle we must overcome.'

But while emphasising his number one priority, he made one thing clear, 'Winning is important, but we must do it with style. After every game I must ask myself, "Are you satisfied?"'

Oxford United: Parks, Langan, Slatter (1), Phillips, Briggs, Shotton, Houghton, Aldridge (1 pen.), Leworthy, Trewick, Brock. Substitute: Reck not used.
Manchester United: Turner, Duxbury, Albiston, Moran, McGrath, Hogg, Blackmore, Moses, Stapleton, Davenport, Barnes. Substitute: Olsen for McGrath.
Score: 1-0
Attendance: 13,545

Alex Ferguson would have been far from satisfied following his first ninety minutes in charge of Manchester United, with the visit to the Manor Ground, Oxford, ending in a 2-0 defeat, and producing headlines such as 'Fergie's Flops – United Hit New Low', 'Misery For Fergie', 'Sad Start For Fergie' and 'Fergie Faces Grim Reality'. It took the new United manager a mere sixteen minutes to realise the enormity of the task that lay in front of him, as by that time his team were already a goal behind.

To be fair, Ferguson's initial team selection was governed more by injuries than personal choice, with Moran, who was given the captaincy, Duxbury, Blackmore and Barnes all coming into the line-up. Oxford pressed forward from the first whistle, while two successive corners in the tenth minute were the best attacking options that the visitors could manage.

With sixteen minutes gone, John Aldridge latched onto the ball following a slip by Blackmore and, as the Oxford No. 8 moved into the United penalty area, he was tripped by Moran, giving the referee no option but to point to the spot. Aldridge took the kick himself and placed it low to the right of Chris Turner to put his team in front. It was his fourteenth goal of the season, only two less than United had managed in their thirteen League outings.

Four minutes later it could well have been 2-0, but only a last-gasp clearance by Duxbury prevented Aldridge from doubling his total as he moved on to a Phillips pass. A Moses clearance was charged down by Aldridge, but the Oxford danger man hurried his shot under pressure, and the opportunity was lost.

It took United almost half an hour before they launched the first of their spasmodic attacks. Davenport, having taken up a position wide on the right, sent the ball into the Oxford penalty area, setting up an ideal opportunity for Stapleton, but what looked like a certain goal saw the ball blocked by Briggs. Barnes shot wide, while Stapleton ballooned yet another opportunity high over the Oxford crossbar.

The United midfield was struggling to support their fellow forwards, but any time United did manage to make leeway towards the Oxford goal, they were submerged by a sea of yellow shirts.

There were cries for a second Oxford penalty as the second half got underway, with Ferguson now having vacated his seat in the directors' box for one in the touchline dugout. A Phillips cross was headed back across the face of the United goal by Leworthy, with the ball striking Duxbury on the arm. It had clearly been unintentional, though, and much to United's relief, the referee waved play on.

Oxford, well aware of the fragility of the United defence and the lack of confidence of the team as a whole, harried and harassed the red shirts at every opportunity. Moran averted certain danger with a rather adventurous back header, while Hogg was spoken to for something of an overenthusiastic challenge on Leworthy. Albiston's embarrassment, following a bad defensive error, was prevented thanks to a fine save from Turner, just as much as the rather poor shot from Leworthy.

Parks in the Oxford goal was seldom troubled, although he was to take two attempts to prevent a Davenport shot from trickling across the line. He also breathed a sigh of relief when a Barnes corner skimmed the heads of everyone encamped in his goalmouth.

As the half progressed, United began to look more settled. Blackmore forced Parks into making a couple of fine saves, firstly from a powerful header and then with a low drive. In midfield, Moses tried to drive his colleagues forward, as Davenport appealed for a penalty after being knocked off the ball.

With fifteen minutes remaining, Ferguson replaced McGrath, who was not enjoying the best of afternoons in a somewhat unfamiliar midfield role, with Olsen, taking something of a gamble – not simply by having Moses and the Dane on the same pitch, but by putting more emphasis on attack rather than defence. Disappointingly, it was not to pay off.

As the clock ticked to the eightieth minute, any thoughts of an equaliser were quickly diminished. Houghton sent the ball out to Brock on the right and the Oxford outside-left crossed hard into the United goalmouth, where Slater slipped the ball past Turner to make it 2-0.

Davenport was the liveliest of the United forwards, but as a team they were sloppy at the back and unproductive in midfield. However, there was some encouragement from Oxford manager Maurice Evans, as he commented after the match to the waiting reporters, 'You should have seen United when they lost 4-1 at Southampton last Tuesday night. They were 100 per cent better today.'

Words, however, were of little encouragement to Alex Ferguson: 'It was always going to be a difficult game but I thought we gave away two bad goals.

'I've learned a few things today, but I am not going to start crticising individuals and I'll see what happens over the next few weeks before I even think about buying new players.'

Somerset Trojans (A)

1 December 1987

It had certainly been an eye-opening ninety minutes at the Manor Ground for Alex Ferguson, and he had much to contemplate as he returned to Aberdeen for the remainder of his weekend. But even just a matter of days into the job, the Glaswegian knew what he wanted from himself and from his players, leaving the latter, and indeed the United support, in no doubt as to what lay ahead.

'You are not fit enough for me,' the players were unceremoniously informed, with Ferguson insisting, 'It will take three or four weeks to get the United players up to the level of fitness I require.'

'Reputations count for nothing with me. And I don't care how big they are. It's performances that impress me. Results. Hard facts. And that's the way it is going to be.

'If I had been the boss when the likes of Bobby Charlton, Denis Law, George Best and Paddy Crerand were here, and they failed to do the business, they'd have been on their way.

'I have a terrible temper. But I've learned to live with it and I know how to make it work for me. I know the players would rather have me praising them for something well done than yelling at them for errors. But if I make them cry because of a mistake, they'll not do it again without risking my wrath. I want them to have enough arrogance to know that if they make a big mistake they can shrug it off because they know they won't repeat it.'

He continued, 'I will make one promise. I'll make sure the fine traditions of United's attacking flair will flourish under me. I love attacking football.

'But it will be done on a firm foundation of strong defence without taking anything away from the attack. I'm going for wins and nobody will see us hanging on for a point. I hate sharing anything, to be second. I was born to be a winner. This club was made for success and I'll get it back on the right lines.

'I hate being second and it won't be for the want of trying and sweating that we won't succeed.'

It did take Alex Ferguson time to get the show on the road, with one goal in his first four fixtures – that one goal bringing his first victory against Queens Park Rangers at Old Trafford – leaving the Old Trafford support wondering if indeed there was going to be any improvement on what they had witnessed under Ron Atkinson. But suddenly there were eight in the following three games, and while they only produced one victory and two draws, a glimmer of light appeared on the distant horizon.

But that glimmer of light suddenly became a flash of lightning and several cracks of thunder, as Ferguson unleashed his infamous temper on a stunned United dressing room at Wimbledon following a 1-0 defeat in the fourth last match of the season. He ranted and raved for a full fifteen minutes, telling his players what he thought of them: 'That was not the kind of performance I expect from Manchester United,' he bellowed. His rant apparently fell on deaf ears though, as they won only one of the remaining three fixtures, and it was obvious he had a job on his hands.

United finished the 1986/87 season eleventh in the First Division, a drop of seven places compared to the previous season, but it would be the following campaign when Ferguson's worth would be judged. The 1987/88 season was still going to be something of a learning curve for the United players, getting to know the manager's ways and ideas and, perhaps more importantly, coming to grips with his Clydeside accent.

As a player, Alex Ferguson, as well as having an eye for goal, was a robust, all-elbows type of forward, giving as good as he got and afraid of no one in the hustle and bustle of football in the fifties and sixties.

If the players were ever in any doubt as to what made the man, having been given a crash course in the 'world according to Alex Ferguson' by Gordon Strachan, who played under him at Aberdeen, then they were left in no doubt as to his 100 per cent total involvement and competitiveness during a mid-season break in Bermuda.

United: Walsh, Knox (1), Albiston, Wilson (1), Moran, Duxbury, Robson, Strachan, McClair (1), Davenport, Olsen (1). Substitutes: Gardner for Moran and Ferguson for Davenport.
Somerset Trojans: No line-up available.
Score: 4-1
Attendance: 2,000

Following the first of the two games, a 4-1 victory over the Bermuda national side, United were suddenly splashed across the front pages, with Clayton Blackmore accused of rape in a nightclub toilet. The Welsh international was locked up in a tiny cell for some thirty-two hours before being cleared of the allegation. The incident was pushed to one side, although Blackmore was not selected for the second of the two games against the Bermudian League champions. But even without Blackmore, who club officials simply said was 'unavailable' in order to keep him away from the media glare, the match still managed to end in controversy, with Alex Ferguson well to the fore.

With the Welshman remaining in the team hotel and injuries to Norman Whiteside and Viv Anderson, United were struggling to make up their numbers, calling on assistant manager Archie Knox to fill the right-back spot and reserve-team player David Wilson taking the No. 4 shirt, with former junior player David Gardner, who was on holiday on the island, and a certain Alex Ferguson making up the substitute bench.

Somerset had hoped to call on George Best to add to their line-up, but the wayward Irishman was delayed back in Belfast as he tried to negotiate a testimonial match in his home city. But even without the former United player, the locals were more than up for the challenge against their big-name opponents.

There was never really much of a chance that something of a shock result could be pulled off, but Brian McClair, Peter Davenport and Bryan Robson all missed good scoring opportunities in the opening stages of the game, prior to rookie David Wilson giving United the lead in the nineteenth minute. Jesper Olsen made it 2-0 prior to the interval, with United well in command.

The Trojans pulled themselves back into the game via the penalty spot in the fifty-seventh minute, Dennis Brown scoring after 'keeper Gary Walsh had been penalised for pushing, but any hopes they began to hold of snatching a creditable draw, or even an unthought-of victory, evaporated completely nine minutes later when Strachan evaded a Somerset defender before finding Olsen, who steered the ball inside to McClair to side-foot home.

Picking up a groin strain, Peter Davenport was taken off and, much to the merriment of the United players, on came Alex Ferguson in his place, the United manager taking up his old familiar forward role.

Ferguson clearly relished the opportunity to get involved in the game and harassed the Somerset defence as often as possible, but much to his disappointment, he could not get his name on the scoresheet and was clearly irked when his assistant manager notched United's fourth, Archie Knox blasting home a superbly hit 35-yard left-footed drive four minutes from time.

The United manager became even more involved in the match, verbally on this occasion, after goalkeeper Gary Walsh was kicked in the head by the onrunning Everett Wellman two minutes from time, as he dived at the Somerset forward's feet.

Such was the ferocity of the kick on the unfortunate 'keeper's head that the Trojans forward had to go to hospital the following morning for an X-ray on his ankle. The United 'keeper had been kept in the same hospital overnight with concussion, an injury that took him a considerable time to get over.

'I didn't really want to play,' said Ferguson later, 'But had to. But after thinking about it, I enjoyed myself. It was a lot of fun. I am in fairly good shape for my age – I've a little pouch but it's not that bad! In fact, I ran a marathon two years ago.'

But what of his number two? 'He played well, didn't he? And that was a cracking goal he scored – he showed he still had it. I know all the players had a good laugh watching Archie and myself out there playing.'

Liverpool (A)

4 April 1988

Only one defeat in the opening fifteen games of the 1986/87 season helped create the belief that, in Alex Ferguson, Manchester United could once again achieve the success at League level that the club so craved.

As the season moved toward its finale, United were clinging onto Liverpool's shirt tails, thanks mainly to the goals of Brian McClair who, along with Viv Anderson, had been Ferguson's first signing for United. The Scot was something of a steal, with Celtic wanting £2 million for his signature, and the United manager gambling on a tribunal setting the fee lower. Ferguson won another victory, with the fee set at £850,000.

With half a dozen games remaining, United were due to travel to Liverpool, with the Anfield men sitting eight points in front. A victory would reduce that lead to five, but whether or not further points could be clawed back was debatable. United could only live in hope.

'The title is still there to be won,' said Ferguson, geeing up his troops for the trip along the East Lancs Road to a ground where they had not lost since Boxing Day 1979.

Liverpool: Grobbelaar, Gillespie (1), Ablett, Nichol, Spackman, Hansen, Beardsley (1), Aldridge, Houghton, Barnes, McMahon (1). Substitute: Johnson for Aldridge.
United: Turner, Anderson, Blackmore, Bruce, McGrath, Duxbury, Robson (2), Strachan (1), McClair, Davenport, Gibson. Substitutes: Olsen for Duxbury and Whiteside for Blackmore.
Score: 3-3
Attendance: 43,497

As always, Anfield was a cauldron of hate, but on this occasion victory for either side held a greater prize.

With the game barely two minutes old and many still making their way onto the already packed terracing, the visitors silenced the Kop by taking the lead.

Gary Gillespie panicked under pressure as three United forwards closed in and gave the ball away, allowing McClair and Davenport to attack the stretched Liverpool defence – the latter sending the ball low across the face of Grobbelaar's goal. Unmarked, in front of goal, Bryan Robson strode forward and from close range gave United the lead.

The goal was like a red rag to a bull. Liverpool sprang to life and it was only the brilliance of Paul McGrath that stood between the home side and goals. The Irishman, however, could only do so much and, on the half-hour, United's defensive barrier collapsed. Houghton escaped the clutches of Robson and, as his cross flew towards the United goal, Beardsley evaded Steve Bruce's tackle to slip the ball past a helpless Turner.

Four minutes before the interval, Liverpool were in front, Beardsley again in the thick of the action. Getting behind the United defence, he glided the ball towards the far post where Barnes was lurking and the England winger hooked the ball back towards the oncoming Gillespie, who made up for his earlier error by out-jumping McGrath and propelling a powerful header past Turner.

Within a minute of the second half getting underway, United were 3-1 behind. Steve McMahon sent a searing drive past Turner from all of 20 yards.

The championship trophy edged closer to the Anfield club.

Sensing the game slipping away, Ferguson decided on one final throw of the dice by sending on Norman Whiteside, along with Jesper Olsen in place of Blackmore and Duxbury in the fifty-fourth minute.

Many felt that the destination of the title was more of a foregone conclusion ten minutes later, when Colin Gibson, already booked for back-heeling the ball away at a free-kick, was sent off for a foul on Steve Nichol.

Olsen's arrival on the scene caused little concern to the Anfield hoards, but upon the sight of Whiteside on the touchline, torrents of abuse had echoed down from all around the ground and it took the big Irishman only a matter of minutes before he found his way into the referee's notebook, increasing his personal abuse a hundredfold, as he initially elbowed Barnes unceremoniously out of the way before leaving McMahon a crumpled heap on the Anfield turf.

Olsen almost pulled a goal back, eluding Spackman before lobbing the ball goalwards, with only an acrobatic backwards leap from Grobbelaar managing to fingertip the ball onto the bar.

But Whiteside was soon to add brain to his brawn as Liverpool, unperturbed by Olsen's earlier attempt on goal, allowed Robson to latch onto Whiteside's pass in the sixty-fifth minute and fire home from 18 yards, with a slight deflection off Gillespie, edging United back into the game.

It was Liverpool who now had their backs to the wall, as United pushed forward and, with thirteen minutes remaining, their defence was once again caught like a rabbit in the glare of the oncoming headlights, freezing as McClair moved forward, pulling defenders away from goal and allowing Davenport to find Strachan, with the ginger-headed Scot holding off Hansen before slipping the ball coolly past Grobbelaar to the heartbreak of the stunned Kop only yards away.

It took a fine Turner save from a Gillespie header to ensure the visitors left Liverpool with a point, but the title was still to prove out of United's grasp.

It was an outcome that Alex Ferguson was still unhappy with.

'I can now understand why clubs go away from here biting their tongues and choking on their own vomit after knowing they have been done by referees.

'I can now understand how they feel, because I feel that today. I am not getting at this particular referee. The whole intimidating atmosphere and the monopoly Liverpool have enjoyed for years gets to them eventually.

'Colin Gibson was sent off for kicking the ball away, which was a stupid thing to do. The actual tackle was not worth a booking because Steve McMahon had been committing fouls all afternoon and got away with them.

'We deserved a result in the end because to have to come from 3-1 down with ten men was quite a task.'

'You might as well talk to my daughter. You'll get more sense out of her,' snapped a passing Dalglish, kickstarting a verbal four-letter-word war. But it was the United manager who had the final word. 'Despite the interruptions from Kenny Dalglish, it has been a good afternoon.'

Wimbledon (H)

2 May 1989

As it was, despite United winning their remaining five fixtures, there was to be no slip up on Merseyside and the First Division championship remained a distant memory, although it was the first time that the runners-up spot had been achieved since 1979/80.

Runners-up to Liverpool in 1987/88 was something of an achievement for Alex Ferguson's team, but it was also something of a false dawn, as they were in hindsight as far away from winning that elusive title for the first time since 1967 as they ever were. It was certainly no stepping stone to success; indeed, it was to prove the exact opposite, with season 1988/89 testing the United manager to the limit.

'Winning the League is an obsession at United and I can understand that feeling after so many years without the title,' exclaimed Ferguson as yet another season dribbled to a halt by the beginning of April. 'But that is not all down to me,' he continued, 'and I'll not let the disappointment of this season dishearten me.'

Five wins out of seven during January and February was not exactly a major achievement, despite one of those being a 3-1 victory over Liverpool, but for a United side in what was something of a transitional period, it could be considered a good run. However, the season as a whole was most definitely not championship-winning, or indeed championship-challenging form, and this was made clearly obvious during the latter weeks of April when the problems surrounding the club came to the fore with defeats against what could be considered the 'also-rans' of the First Division in Derby County (2-0 at home), Charlton Athletic (1-0 away) and Coventry City (1-0 at home). The latter of the trio had seen a bedraggled United booed off the pitch by the few supporters who had remained until the bitter end.

Dave Sexton had been sacked by a vote from the terraces, due to a mixture of complaints about the style of play and the number of empty seats around the stadium.

Taking both of those into account, Alex Ferguson's days were on the verge of being numbered.

United: Leighton, Duxbury, Donaghy, Bruce, McGrath, Whiteside, Robson, Beardsmore, McClair (1), Hughes, Martin. Substitutes: Maiorana for Whiteside. Blackmore not used.

Wimbledon: Segers, Joseph, Clement, Jones, Young, Scales, Kruszynski, Miller, Gayle, Sanchez, Wise. Substitutes: Cotterell for Miller and Cork for Gayle.
Score: 1-0
Attendance: 23,368 (or approx. 17,000!)

The visit of Wimbledon to Manchester on Tuesday 2 May was as clear an indication as anything that the United manager was indeed living on borrowed time, with his team having recorded only one victory in the last ten games. The south London side did not register highly on the entertainment charts, nor did they have much of a travelling support. They did, however, rely on 100 per cent commitment and rough, sometimes underhand tactics to survive and cajole opponents. None of those could be used as an excuse for an Old Trafford attendance that wasn't simply poor, but something of a warning to the board and management that the natives were far from happy.

Given officially as 23,368, the attendance was reported at the time as being the lowest for a League match down Warwick Road for eighteen years, but the match in question was against West Bromwich Albion and had actually been played at Stoke City's Victoria Ground, due to Old Trafford being closed by the Football Association. The attendance was in reality some 6,000 fewer, as United had taken into account all season ticket holders, not simply those who had bothered to turn up. No matter; it was still the lowest home attendance since 9 May 1966, when 23,039 turned up to watch Aston Villa beaten 6-1.

For those who bothered to turn up, they had to endure an evening described by Ian Ross of the *Guardian* as 'The alienation of a once proud team from its disenchanted public, when Old Trafford, the so called "Theatre of Dreams" played host to a footballing equivalent of an end-of-the-pier show.'

United's play in the opening stages of the game, was 'littered with the sort of schoolboy errors which have become commonplace in recent weeks'. Rarely did any real excitement bubble over, with the slow handclapping the only real noise to echo around the sparkly populated stadium. Booing and chants of 'rubbish' were also regularly heard, but with United having failed to score in the previous four games, goals were always going to be few and far between.

Jim Leighton had to be alert early on as Sanchez shot from close in, while Steve Bruce was booed after twenty-two minutes for passing the ball back to his 'keeper rather than kicking it forward. However, there was a ripple of excitement as Bryan Robson moved forward, with his cross beating Segers in the Wimbledon goal, before falling at the feet of Whiteside. On another day, the Irishman would have scored, but tonight, Scales was ideally placed to clear off the line.

Prior to the interval, Mal Donaghy broke through from midfield, but his effort cannoned off the crossbar and away to safety.

Despite the occasional attack, there were also hints of nervousness and, on one occasion, McGrath and Leighton collided as they both went for the ball at the same time following a Wimbledon throw-in.

The second half was little better than the first and the visitors missed an ideal opportunity to take the lead when Cork back-headed to the feet of Miller, but from 3 yards out, he fired wide.

Ferguson rejuggled his troops in an effort to find the required breakthrough, with McGrath pushed up front to partner Whiteside and Hughes. The game dragged on and the meagre crowd grew even less as the minutes ticked away, and how many were still there to see Brian McClair's last-minute goal is anyone's guess. The former Celtic man latched on to the ball and fired past Segers after McGrath's header from Martin's free-kick had been only been parried by the Wimbledon 'keeper.

'It was an eerie experience and nobody wants a repeat of it,' said the United manager after the match. 'It has been a tremendous reminder to the players that if they don't perform to expectations people will stay away.

'It also showed the importance of Manchester United winning while entertaining – and it demonstrated just how quickly fortunes change.'

Wimbledon's Laurie Sanchez also took a swipe at the bedraggled club, saying, 'United talk about the title the whole time but they have not produced the goods for twenty-two years.

'They are a huge club with phenomenal support and should be doing far better. Their fans deserve the best and they are not getting it.

'The game was dead all the way through until the final minutes when they started attacking with a bit of spirit. If changes are not made, United will go through the same thing next season.'

Manchester City (A)

23 September 1989

Whether or not Alex Ferguson would be there next season was up for debate, as the following three fixtures saw Southampton, Queens Park Rangers and Everton all beat United, with newspaper speculation hinting that the Scot could be replaced in the summer by Howard Kendall, currently manager of Everton, with 'several senior figures at Old Trafford dissatisfied with Ferguson'.

Former United boss Tommy Docherty, never short of a few words, proclaimed that Ferguson 'was showing serious signs of mental fatigue' and that he had 'to change his hard-line approach. If he doesn't then the players won't perform for him.

'And if they don't perform, he won't get results. And if he doesn't get results the crowd will stay away.

'And if that continues to happen, either Alex will resign – or he'll get the sack.'

It wasn't simply at first-team level that the club was struggling. If the United first team thought they had it rough, with the disgruntled support and a manager on their back demanding results and improved performances, then they did not have the worries of the second string, with United's reserve side one defeat away from relegation to the Second Division of the Central League.

To guarantee their safety, the United manager played nine players with first-team experience, with the likes of McClair, Blackmore and Bruce augmenting the usual younger-looking line-up.

The 1989/90 season kicked off in spectacular fashion at a sun-kissed Old Trafford, with the 4-1 victory over Arsenal somewhat overshadowed by Michael Knighton's prematch ball-juggling antics in front of the packed Stretford End.

With Martin Edwards looking to sell his shareholding in the club, Knighton had appeared out of the blue with a proposal to buy the club, but as time would tell, he did not have the finance to do so and a seat on the board was the best he could manage.

It was not, however, just Knighton who was to fall by the wayside, as the 4-1 victory over the Gunners was followed by a draw (1-1 against Crystal Palace) and a trio of defeats against Derby County (2-0 away), Norwich City (2-0 at home) and Everton (3-2 away). Newly promoted Millwall were hammered 5-1, while new signings Paul Ince and Danny Wallace scored in the 3-2 Littlewoods Cup defeat of Portsmouth, but a 'derby' encounter against neighbours City loomed on the horizon.

In the Manchester Metro News *on the eve of the game, Tony Lanigan wrote, 'His [Ferguson's] £10-million investment in the team must start paying dividends and after the 5-1 thrashing of Millwall followed by the first-leg cup win, the fans want to see evidence that the championship march really has begun.*

'The team could give them no greater proof than a hammering of City who have rarely been so vulnerable.

'On recent performances and individual quality United should succeed.'

There was indeed to be a hammering, but Lanigan was slightly off the mark.

Manchester City: Cooper, Fleming, Hinchcliffe (1), Bishop (1), Gayle, Redmond, White, Morley (1), Oldfield (2), Brightwell, Lake. Substitutes: Beckford for Lake. Megson not used.

United: Leighton, Anderson, Donaghy, Duxbury, Phelan Pallister, Beardsmore, Ince, McClair, Hughes (1), Wallace. Substitutes: Sharpe for Beardsmore. Blackmore not used.

Score: 5-1

Attendance: 43,246

Two Manchester City goals within the space of a minute in a trouble-strewn 111th 'derby' fixture didn't simply stun United, but knocked them completely off their game. So much so that many of those United supporters who had infiltrated the City section of the North Stand, kicking off a mini-riot within minutes of the match kicking off, had left the vicinity of Maine Road well before the full-time whistle.

It was one of those games when the Bryan Robson syndrome kicked in big style, with the United captain out of the game with a shin injury and the eleven red shirts clearly short of someone to both guide and inspire them through what should have been a comfortable ninety minutes.

The game was disrupted almost immediately after kick-off when a mini-riot erupted in the North Stand with a mass brawl between both sets of supporters, and large numbers of spectators escaped the violence by clambering onto the pitch. Referee Neil Midgley quickly took both teams off the pitch until the police managed to get everything under control, with a large number of United followers moved into a no-man's segregation area.

The trouble was believed to have been pre-planned and ticket touts and City turnstile attendants were blamed for the United fans being in the rival section. The turnstile assistants were believed to have failed to give out ticket vouchers to supporters at City's previous home game and were instead selling them to the touts, allowing them to purchase the tickets for sale on the black market.

Twenty-six were arrested and thirty-seven ejected. Those United supporters among them should have been grateful!

Play eventually resumed eight minutes later and it was City who quickly settled, taking the lead in the eleventh minute, when Hinchcliffe floated the ball out to White on the right, the City winger beating Duxbury with ease before crossing into the United area, where Pallister missed the ball, allowing Oldfield to pounce and put City in front.

Within a minute, it was 2-0, City on this occasion attacking down the left and, with the United defence given no time to muster, Morley beat Leighton after both he and Lake had seen shots blocked.

New boys Ince and Wallace both looked sharp and capable of causing City problems, but the home defence dealt confidently with everything the red shirts threw at them. Beardsmore's cross was met by Pallister, but the central defender's effort was headed off the line by Hinchcliffe.

Redmond cleared from Wallace, while a Beardsmore and Ince forward surge was halted by the well-organised City defence, who were not even put off their game when a goalmouth scramble ensued and it looked as though McClair had forced the ball over the line before Fleming cleared, but the referee, despite appeals, waved play on.

City seemed to grow in confidence and increased their lead in the thirty-sixth minute. Oldfield surged down United's left and once again Pallister was caught out as Bishop strode forward to head past Leighton.

Hughes should have done better when through on goal, but finished poorly, leaving the United support unusually silent as the half-time whistle blew.

United stepped up their game as the second forty-five minutes got underway, no doubt fortified by a pleasant half-time chat with their manager, and six minutes after the restart pulled a goal back. Beardsmore turned past Hinchcliffe before crossing from the right into the city penalty area, where Mark Hughes launched himself into mid-air and volleyed home in spectacular fashion.

Wallace then went close as United again surged forward, Cooper saving at full stretch, but within seven minutes of Hughes scoring, City were again three goals in front. Sloppy defensive play by United once again allowed the home side to capitalise, with Lake creating the opening and Oldfield snapping up the simple opportunity.

Without the inspirational Robson, United were a shambles.

'Easy, easy,' chanted the City support, and indeed it was – more so following the fifth goal, when White crossed for Hinchcliffe to score – and their 'Ferguson out' chants were echoed in some respect by their United counterparts.

It had been a defensive nightmare for United, with neither the full-backs nor the central defenders being able to cope with the slick-moving City side. There had not been five goals scored by either side in a 'derby' match since the 1960/61 season, when United defeated City at Old Trafford and it was the first time that City had scored five against their across-town rivals in thirty-five years.

Humiliation was only the half of it.

'It was like climbing a glass mountain,' said Ferguson after the match. 'That was the worst defensive display I have been involved in. I don't think Jim Leighton has ever conceded five goals. Now I want to sit down and just fathom out what went wrong.'

Having endured a far from comfortable Saturday evening, Ferguson told David Meek of the *Manchester Evening News*, 'None of us must ever forget this derby result.

'It's not a very happy memory, but it must be remembered and used as a driving force to make sure nothing like it ever occurs again.

'I believe it was a freak result, but nevertheless it is in the record books and we have got to make amends.

'It was the worst experience of my football life and the worst result. I have watched the film of the match all weekend and defensively we had a nightmare. City's goals were so simple.

'None of us must forget. As I say we must make the experience work for us to make sure we never ever go through anything like it again.

'It's been a nightmare for me, but we will come through it stronger. I promise.'

Nottingham Forest (A)

7 January 1990

'Believe me, what I have felt in the last week you wouldn't think should happen in football,' said a deflated Alex Ferguson in an interview with Hugh McIlvanney of the Sunday Times a few days after that fateful Saturday. 'Every time somebody looks at me, I feel I betrayed that man. After such a result, you feel as if you have to sneak round corners, feel as if you are some kind of criminal.

'But that's only because you care, care about the people who support you. At Manchester United you become one of them, you think like supporter. They have been waiting twenty-two years for a League championship. I've been waiting less than three but in terms of frustration it seems like twenty-two already.

'There's been a lot of speculation in certain papers over the last few days about my position at Old Trafford, some of it going as far as to link Howard Kendall with my job. At the very least it's been unsettling and at its worst it's been really mischievous. But I mean to be here, making a success of things, three years from now. I know I have the courage to deal with all the sniping but you worry about the effects on your family.'

He continued, 'We have a well-structured youth policy that is at the heart of our operation but young talent must be introduced carefully, in stages, not sucked dry prematurely by over-exposure.

'There were signs of what we could be when we beat Millwall 5-1. There was the look of goals about everything we did and that's how Manchester United should be. It was sickening to be hit with the same scoreline a week later, but we can take positive lessons from that disaster.

'I certainly don't regret for a moment asking Martin Edwards to go into the red to buy big in the summer. I said, "We have to go for broke, we have to show that we want to win the League, that we are not going to accept Liverpool's dominance."'

Thankfully, Michael Knighton's abortive takeover plans took Alex Ferguson's turmoil away from both the front and back pages, but it certainly could not alter the First Division table, which showed Manchester United as being third from bottom, one point above Charlton Athletic and two above Sheffield Wednesday.

The visit of the bottom club, under the managership of Ron Atkinson, to Old Trafford on 14 October could not hide the frustration of the support as to how low the club had fallen, as a poor United side were booed off the pitch following an inept and goalless display.

'I think Fergie will be lucky to last until Christmas,' said Tommy Docherty, while a Daily Telegraph *article by Colin Gibson (not the United player, I must add) was entitled, 'On the third anniversary of his succession, Manchester United's least successful manager in modern history is still keeping the supporters waiting – why Ferguson is running out of false dawns.'*

The article began, 'There was a conspicuous absence of celebrations at Manchester United this week to mark the third anniversary of Alex Ferguson's arrival as manager.

'Old Trafford is hardly in the mood for parties at the moment. Instead, the dwindling numbers who used to pack the terraces are suffering in silence.' It began and ended with, 'The crowd, or what remains of it, is becoming rapidly disillusioned. Old Trafford was once, with its cacophony of noise, the theatre of English football. It has now become the house of broken dreams.

'They are fed up with excuses and of false dawns. Old Trafford needs success and it needs it quickly, otherwise the pressure Mr Ferguson has experienced will grow much worse.'

A 2-1 home defeat by Crystal Palace on 9 December, in front of the lowest Old Trafford crowd of the season – 33,514 – did little to help the United manager's cause, with the Daily Telegraph's *reporter William Johnson penning, 'Brian Clough's talented Nottingham Forest side effectively ended Manchester United's season last March with an FA Cup quarter-final victory at Old Trafford. If they repeat that conquest as the third-round stage next month they may end more than just another disappointing United season.*

'Alex Ferguson, the latest big name manager to suffer under the strain of trying to end an embarrassing wait for an eighth championship, will surely fail in that quest after another surprise defeat – this time against struggling Crystal Palace – emphasised his team's woeful inconsistency.

'His only hope of success, and probably salvation, is in the one-off world of the cup but how fate seems to be conspiring against him. Nobody relishes a tie at the City Ground, least of all a man on borrowed time.'

In the run up to the Forest cup tie, a 3-0 Boxing Day defeat at Villa Park added to Alex Ferguson's woe. 'Condemned,' proclaimed the headline in Today, *while the* Express *went with 'Fergie's Last Stand – Cup flop will be the end'.*

'Everyone seems to have set the cup tie as my trial,' said the manager under the microscope. 'I can cope with that because I know I am doing the job the right way and the motivation of the players is no problem.

'We simply have to get on with it and remember the match will be as hard for Forest as it will be for us.'

In the Sunday Mirror *on the day of the awaited visit to the City Ground, their heading drifted away from the norm with 'Carry On Fergie' and alongside Ken Montgomery quoted Bobby Charlton as saying, 'Alex Ferguson will get on and do his job this weekend and nothing special will happen at Old Trafford on Monday morning whether we win, lose or draw against Forest.*

'Obviously we'd all be bloody sick if we did lose, including Alex. But we are treating this game as we do every game. All this talk of trial by television is nonsense.

'And all those people assuming it are wrong!'

Charlton continued, 'He is a good manager and I just hope that all those people who currently doubt him will realise that when he does start winning things at United.'

Nottingham Forest: Sutton, Laws, Pearce, Walker, Chettle, Hodge, Crosby, Parker, Clough, Jemson, Orlgsson. Substitutes: Charles for Laws and Wilson for Orlgsson.
United: Leighton, Anderson, Martin, Bruce, Phelan, Pallister, Beardsmore, Blackmore, McClair, Hughes, Robins (1). Substitutes: Duxbury for Beardsmore. Milne not used.
Score: 1-0
Attendance: 23,072

The City ground was packed, with unrecorded numbers glued to their television sets, many with divided loyalties, some wanting United to win, while others wanted the victory but the manager sacked nonetheless.

Not only was talisman Bryan Robson missing from the United line-up, but £5.5 million of talent in Ince, Wallace and Webb were also sidelined, making Alex Ferguson's hopes of victory, and perhaps of saving his job, even more delicate than ever before.

During the warm-up, television pundit Jimmy Hill told the watching audience that 'United did not look like a team who had come to do a job'. But as the game got underway, United were adventurous in their play, pushing forward at every opportunity, gaining several corners where they attempted to utilise the aerial power of Pallister and Anderson. It was, however, a risky game to play, as Forest were always dangerous on the counter-attack.

The opening forty-five minutes did little to keep those watching on television awake following their Sunday lunch, with the huge United support on the banks of the Trent left biting their nails as the game unfolded.

As early as the thirteenth minute, Mark Robins showed signs that he might cause the Forest defence a few problems as the game wore on, the diminutive forward turning quickly onto a Martin pass, only to see Sutton in the Forest goal leap to thwart the danger.

'Fergie, Fergie on the dole,' chanted the Forest support, with television close-ups capturing a tense-looking United manager on the touchline, as Phelan, Pallister and Hughes held things together and forced Forest out of creating any form of rhythm. It was clearly a battle for survival from the visitors as they continued to subdue their hosts in midfield, and it was with much relief that they went in at the interval on level terms.

United kept up their momentum after the break and Anderson saw a header saved by Sutton, while Robins, set up by Hughes, hesitated momentarily, and the opportunity was gone. But within ten minutes of the second half getting underway, the tie was turned on its head.

Out on the left near the touchline, Lee Martin dispossessed Orlygsson, moving the ball forward to Hughes, the Welshman proceeding to curl the ball forward and into the Forest penalty area with the outside of his right foot. The quality of the pass caught the Forest defence flatfooted and, as it bounced in front of Sutton, in stooped Robins to head firmly past the Forest 'keeper to give United the advantage.

Now on the back foot, Forest struggled to get back into the game. In midfield, Phelan continued to subdue his opposite numbers, with Bruce and Pallister behind him keeping the ever-threatening Nigel Clough under control. Hughes surged through on goal, but thoughts of a second goal were dismissed by an excellent tackle from Walker.

Play began to flow from end to end and Pallister had to head away from Crosby, suddenly appearing at the opposite end where his header grazed the forest crossbar. When Forest did manage to attack the United goal, they found Leighton in inspired form. The 'keeper was beaten by a Jemson header from a Parker free-kick but, much to United's relief, a linesman's flag alerted the referee to the Forest man being in an offside position. Jemson also shot wide from only 6 yards out, dragging another effort across the face of the United goal.

It was clearly not going to be Forest's day when Nigel Clough was wrestled to the ground by Pallister twelve minutes from time, only to see the referee wave play on.

When Les Shapter eventually blew his whistle to signal the end of the game, a much relieved Alex Ferguson dashed from the dugout to embrace match-winning Robins. It was a goal that would be written into the Manchester United history books, never mind the record books.

'Those last fifteen minutes are when you age,' proclaimed the United manager after the game. 'In those fifteen minutes today it was eyes shut and praying. That's the time you need luck. Today we got the breaks. That's the difference ... there's been a lot of pressure but I don't want to get into the personal thing [this was reference to the criticism that had come his way from Tommy Docherty and George Best].

'We are an inspirational club. Next Saturday we'll have a huge crowd. They become inspired by the type of thing that happened today.'

10

Crystal Palace (N)

17 May 1990

Despite clearing that precarious 'job saving' hurdle that was Forest, speculation over Alex Ferguson's future just would not go away. A 2-0 defeat at Carrow Road Norwich left United only four points off the bottom of the First Division, with a mere two points separating the three clubs above bottom-placed Charlton. Bookmakers William Hill had United as 5-2 for the drop.

Hereford were defeated 1-0 in the fourth round of the cup; Newcastle United, again away from home, were overcome 3-2 in a thrilling encounter. But sandwiched in between and as equally important was a 2-1 victory at Millwall, ending a dismal run of twelve games without a League victory, the worst run in the club's history since 1930/31.

Again on the road, a solitary Brian McClair goal at Bramall Lane Sheffield took United into the FA Cup semi-finals, where a local derby against Oldham Athletic at Maine Road awaited.

A thrilling, end-to-end 3-3 draw saw the unfancied Oldham force United into a replay, and back at Maine Road three days later it was Mark Robins who once again became Alex Ferguson's lucky mascot with an extra-time winner with the score poised at 1-1.

In the League, United continued to stutter along, but thankfully other clubs in the same relegation-haunted position did likewise and, as the campaign dwindled to a close, United were five points clear of the drop. It was something of a mirror image of the 1962/63 season, when the club was troubled for long spells with a drop into Division Two, while marching to Wembley where, albeit as underdogs, they defeated Leicester City.

So it was to Wembley in May, with Crystal Palace, who had defeated Liverpool in the other semi-final, lying in wait. Many felt that it was a foregone conclusion that United would stride to victory, but they were soon to discover that it was far from it.

United went behind in almost comic fashion, a Palace free-kick pinballing around the United area before it was prodded over the line either by O'Reilly or a Pallister touch. Robson's equaliser was just as debatable, as it deflected off Pemberton's shin, but there was no doubting the authenticity of United's second from Hughes.

The introduction of Wright galvanised Palace and he put them level in the seventy-third minute and in front in the second minute of extra time. Mark Hughes was to save United's blushes in the 113th minute, robbing United old boy Steve Coppell, the Palace manager, of a memorable victory.

United: Sealey, Ince, Martin (1), Bruce, Phelan, Pallister, Robson, Webb, McClair Hughes, Wallace. Substitutes: Robins and Blackmore – both unused.
Crystal Palace: Martyn, Pemberton, Shaw, Gray, O'Reilly, Thorn, Barber, Thomas, Bright, Salako, Pardew. Substitutes: Wright for Barber and Madden for Salako.
Score: 1-0
Attendance: 80,000

Shaken by the result, and indeed his team's overall performance, Alex Ferguson had much to deliberate before the following Thursday's replay and, after much heart searching, he decided to drop his former Aberdeen goalkeeper Jim Leighton, who had endured a torrid afternoon beneath the twin towers in the first encounter against Palace. In his place came on-loan Luton Town's Les Sealey, but the prematch announcement of his name over the tannoy was greeted by surprise and boos from the United section of the stadium.

The ninety minutes that unfolded were a far cry from the first encounter, as the replay turned out to be something of a spiteful and physical battle, with Stuart Jones in the *Times* writing that it 'bordered on the disgraceful' and that 'there were so many ugly and illegitimate assaults that the national stadium resembled an unlit back-street alley'.

Palace, sensing that they would be up against an entirely different United than in the first encounter, set their stall out accordingly and attacked United, in more ways than one, from the offset, with the stand-in 'keeper coming in for closer attention than most.

Bright, who had fouled Bruce as early as the third minute, mounted something of a physical assault on Sealey, who was playing in only his third game for the club, catching him in the midriff with an unsavoury challenge. Pardew threw the ball into McClair's face and soon afterwards was fortunate not to be sent off with a late challenge on Ince. All this was in the opening twenty minutes, with little in the way of actual football having been played.

Sealey saved from Salako in the twenty-third minute as Palace pressed forward, forgetting momentarily the physical side of their game and two minutes later managing to get his body behind a Gray free-kick after Bruce had handled on the outside of the area. In the scramble that followed, Ince looked to have fouled a Palace player, but the referee waved away the Londoners' appeals.

A sneaky elbow from Hughes caught O'Reilly in some form of retaliation for the rather underhand tactics of the Palace players, who almost received punishment of a more significant form, but Webb's free-kick hit the side netting.

United slowly began to put their game together, forgetting the ulterior motives of their opponents, but the first half was to remain goalless, although they did manage to pick up where they left off as the second forty-five minutes got underway, with Hughes, collecting the ball on the right, sending over an inviting cross towards McClair, only for the head of O'Reilly to divert the ball away.

The physical side of the game continued with Salako flattening Wallace and Thorn, who rather bravely fouled Hughes, for which he was booked, but they were to receive their comeuppance almost on the hour mark, when United deservingly took the lead.

Neil Webb, picking the ball up halfway inside the Palace half, spotted full-back Lee Martin making ground down the opposite flank, leaving the Palace right-back Pemberton in his wake. With pinpoint accuracy, Webb picked out his red-shirted teammate with a 30-yard cross-field ball and, having chested the ball down as he continued to move forward, Martin fired the ball high into the roof of the Palace net, giving 'keeper Martyn no chance.

Coppell threw to Wright in the hope that he might, as he had done in the first meeting, change the course of the game, and within six minutes they did come close to an equaliser when Gray got a foot to the ball amid a goalmouth scramble, but Sealey once again kept the ball out.

Twelve minutes from time, Robson rose above the Palace defence to meet Webb's free-kick. But the goal that would have sealed victory failed to materialise as the ball bounced of the Palace crossbar with Martyn well beaten.

United managed to hold on to their solitary-goal advantage, lifting the FA Cup for a record seventh time, in a season that could well have developed into controversy and mayhem had the United board listened to the calls from the terraces, as they had done before, and sacked Alex Ferguson.

Surprisingly, the United manager had little to say following his first taste of silverware south of the border. 'This is the greatest day of my life' was basically it, but he was full of praise for both goalscorer Lee Martin and stand-in 'keeper Les Sealy. On the man whose goal secured victory, he said, 'It was a marvellous ball and a marvellous finish. I'm delighted for him. He has been our best player this season and grew up today.'

On the subject of leaving his first-choice goalkeeper out of the starting line-up, he refused to be drawn, saying simply, 'I don't want to talk about Leighton. That's my business.' He was later to add, 'I knew the decision would be controversial but, more importantly, I knew it was right.'

11

Barcelona (N)

15 May 1991

The Heysel Stadium disaster on 29 May 1985, which saw thirty-nine Juventus supporters killed and a further 600 injured prior to the European Cup final against Liverpool in Brussels, led to all English clubs being banned from European competitions by UEFA for an indefinite period of time.

This ban was lifted in the summer of 1990, Liverpool being excluded for an additional year, but only to allow United, as FA Cup winners, and Aston Villa, as runners-up in the First Division, to compete in the European Cup Winners' Cup, a competition that they should have been involved in back in 1985, having defeated Everton in that season's final and the UEFA Cup respectively. During that five-year ban, United should also have been involved in the UEFA Cup on two occasions: in 1986/87 after finishing fourth in the First Division and again in 1988/89 after finishing as runners-up.

Their return to European football saw them paired with the unknown Hungarian side Pécsi Munkás in the first round, with a 3-0 aggregate victory pairing them with nearer-to-home Wrexham in round two. The Welsh side were defeated 5-0 over the two legs, while United conceded their first goal in the competition against Montpellier at home in the quarter-final 1-1 draw. A 2-0 victory in France took them into the semi-finals where Legia Warsaw lay in wait. A 3-1 win in Poland was more or less enough to book United a place in the final, with the 1-1 home draw nothing but a mere formality.

If the opponents en route to the final were little more than minor attractions on the European circuit, there was nothing small-time about Barcelona, who stood between United and their first European success since 1968.

United: Sealey, Irwin, Blackmore, Bruce, Phelan, Pallister, Robson, Ince, McClair, Hughes (2), Sharpe. Substitutes: Walsh, Donaghy, Webb, Robins, Wallace – all unused.
Barcelona: Busquets, Nando, Alexanco, Koeman (1), Ferrer, Bakero, Goicoechea, Eusebio, Salinas, Laudrup, Beguiristain. Substitutes: Pinilla for Alexanco. Anjoy, Serna, Soler, and Herrera not used.
Score: 2-1
Attendance: 50,000

From the 5-1 nightmare at Maine Road and the haunting cries of 'Fergie Out' floating around the far-from-full Old Trafford via an FA Cup final victory beneath Wembley's twin towers, few would have imagined that within a couple of years they would be assembled on foreign soil to watch the famous red shirts once again compete in a major European final.

The pouring rain did little to dispel the euphoric feeling of the huge United support – perhaps it felt like home to them – nor did have any effect on Alex Ferguson's team, an XI that did not include Neil Webb, his place given to Mike Phelan, a decision that was to be justified as the night wore on.

On the rain-sodden pitch, play in the opening stages was cautious due to both the conditions and neither side wanting to give the other any early advantage. As early as the fifth minute, United had their opponents on the defensive, Ince, McClair and Robson combining to send Sharpe away down the right. Outrunning Nando on the left, the winger managed to force a corner, but from the kick, the ball was cleared.

Phelan, who was to prove that his manager's decision to play him was correct, sent an inviting ball into the Barcelona area and, with the 'keeper moving off his line, Hughes looked like taking the ball in his stride. But before he could reach it, he was upended by Nando, who was relieved that the referee allowed play to continue.

Both Gary Pallister and Les Sealey had passed late fitness tests and it was the United centre-half who sent McClair scurrying through the Spanish defence, but as debutant Busquets advanced from his line, the Scot lifted his shot high over the bar.

It was well into the half before the United defence were put under any sort of pressure. Laudrup, always a danger, sent a shot wide of the post and it was not until two minutes before the interval that Sealey was called upon to make his first save as Goicoechea shot straight at him. At the opposite end, as half-time beckoned, Blackmore sent a free-kick off target after Hughes had been fouled by Alexanco.

Slowly United began to take control of the game, sensing that Barcelona's reputation was worse than their bite, but by half-time they had failed to put the nervous Busquets under any real pressure.

As the second half got underway, Salinas slipped past Bruce inside the United area, but before he could cause any real danger, Ince had robbed him off the ball. Then, at the opposite end, Sharpe once again got the better of Nando, but not for the first time was brought crashing to the ground. Hughes was only inches away from connecting with Blackmore's free-kick.

There were countless flashes of individual brilliance, but actual teamwork seldom flourished and, as the game wore on, play became more cautious and it became more likely that any goal would come from a dead-ball situation.

On the hour, a sliced clearance from a Barcelona defender hung in the wind and, under pressure from McClair, Busquets managed to punch clear the ball. However, he only managed to go as far as Sharpe, but the winger's shot, from a difficult angle, smacked into the side netting.

Eight minutes later, the deadlock was finally broken.

Hughes was brought down by Alexanco to the left of the Barcelona area and, as Robson's free-kick swung towards goal, Busquets began to make a hopeful move for the ball; it began to swerve away from him, catching the 'keeper in two minds. Bruce headed the ball past the stranded 'keeper and, as it was about to cross the line, Hughes hammered the ball home.

Within five minutes, the Spaniards were two down. Robson caught the Barcelona defence square with an angled pass to Hughes. Spotting the immediate danger, Busquets raced from his goal, but was once again left stranded as the Welshman moved past him before driving the ball into the far corner from a narrow angle.

It was sweet revenge for the United man against his former employers.

Although well in command, there were still a few anxious moments in the minutes that remained; even more so when Koeman pulled a goal back in the seventy-ninth minute, his free-kick deceiving Sealey. Hughes came close to claiming a hat-trick in the dying minutes, but was brought down by Nando on the edge of the penalty area. It was a tackle that bought the robust Spanish defender a red card.

'Always Look on the Bright Side of Life' echoed around the stadium as the final minutes ticked away and amid the display of red, black and white flags, from as far afield as Malta and Middleton, the final whistle was greeted with a crescendo of noise from the vast United contingent as they celebrated yet another European success for Manchester United.

12

Queens Park Rangers (H)
1 January 1992

For Alex Ferguson, his second trophy in two years was a platform for further success. 'I can't say we will win the League next season,' he said, 'but I certainly hope we will be up there alongside Liverpool.

'Success can do many things and one of the benefits is that it gives you stature and it gives you a presence.

'When Liverpool were at their peak they won games simply because they were Liverpool and teams feared them. Their name won them games. We have not reached that stage but we can use last night to give ourselves an authority.

'We must demand more of ourselves. The experience of winning in Rotterdam will help because everyone recognises that it was a great achievement for the players.'

Being a cup team, and in reality that was all this United side was, did bring recognition to the club, and of course much coveted silverware, but the sought-after crown was the League championship.

'They (the supporters) have a right to want that,' Ferguson stressed. 'The title is a conflict that we must become involved in. We must begin to change that now and we are developing into championship material. What we have to do is create the feeling in our side that we have the will to win all our games.

'We don't want to create monsters for ourselves – we must prove we can play against lesser sides as well as top teams. We didn't do that last season.

'We will be better next season. I am convinced of that.'

The championship challenge that Alex Ferguson talked about following the success in Rotterdam was not simply a figment of his imagination or a morale-boosting speech in an effort to galvanise his troops – it was something that became a reality. Indeed, the 1991/92 season could have seen that elusive League title finding its way to Old Trafford, had it not been for something else that the United manager had mentioned following the victory against Barcelona.

'We can beat the best and lose to the worst' were his words and this was to turn out rather prophetic as United could only manage the runners-up spot, finishing three points behind Leeds United.

United: Schmeichel, Parker, Blackmore, Bruce, Webb, Pallister, Phelan, Ince, McClair (1), Hughes, Sharpe. Substitutes: Giggs for Phelan. Donaghy not used.

Queens Park Rangers: Stejskal, Bardsley, Wilson, Wilkins, Peacock, McDonald, Holloway, Barker, Bailey (3), Wegrie, Stinton (1). Substitutes: Penrice and Tilson – both not used.

Score: 4-1

Attendance: 38,554

It had certainly been a Merry Christmas down Old Trafford way. Chelsea had been beaten 3-1 at Stamford Bridge on 15 December, while Oldham Athletic were hammered 6-3 on Boxing Day. Title rivals Leeds United had been held to a 1-1 draw at Elland Road on the 29th, a result that left United sitting on top of the First Division table, two points ahead of the Yorkshire side, with two games in hand.

The visit of Queens Park Rangers to Old Trafford on the first day of the New Year should have been little more than a formality for United, but it was to turn into something of a nightmare. Leeds, having kicked off earlier and beaten West Ham United 3-1, now held a one-point advantage, but the lowest Old Trafford crowd of the season expected their favourites to regain top spot with a fluent display against the Londoners, who trailed them by some eighteen points.

United began shabbily, as if suffering a hangover from the previous night's celebrations, and found themselves 2-0 behind after only five minutes. With only three minutes on the clock and many still making their way into the ground, Blackmore's attempted tackle on Wegerie was little more than a token gesture and the Rangers man drifted down the right before finding Barker, who in turn prodded the ball to the unmarked Stinton, who had all the time in the world to beat Schmeichel.

Two minutes later, Stinton was again in the thick of things, on this occasion creating the opportunity for Bailey to score. The tall centre-forward shielded the ball from the totally ineffective Blackmore, who was only included due to an injury to Irwin, before shooting for goal. His effort, although partially blocked by the arm of the advancing Schmeichel, was allowed to roll over the line.

The visitors had the United defence all over the place, never allowing them the opportunity to settle. Holloway drove narrowly over the crossbar, while Bailey, running onto a ball lobbed forward from Peacock, saw his effort go narrowly over.

As the interval arrived, United had failed to muster a solitary effort on goal and left the pitch to the accompaniment of boos. But, shaken from a half-time talking-to from their manager, they showed slightly more interest in the proceedings as the second half got underway, with both Hughes and Blackmore having awoken from their slumbers, bringing the previously bored Stejskal into the action. But there were only sporadic attacks on the visitor's goal, as Rangers were soon to resume where they had left off, comfortably pressing United on the counter-attack.

In the fifty-eighth minute, United were three behind. Stinton again split the United defence with a finely measured through ball, which Bruce failed to cut out and Bailey once again had little difficulty in beating Schmeichel with a precise lob.

United were abysmal and their performance and the game in general had become something of an embarrassment. Even a McClair goal eight minutes from time, having previously had another effort disallowed, did little to stir the crowd, or what was left of it, and four minutes later there was a mad dash for the exit gates as Bailey made it 4-1.

Stinton beat Blackmore on the halfway line and charged forward unchallenged. Choosing not to tackle, Pallister paid more attention to Bailey, allowing Stinton to shoot. Schmeichel managed to turn the ball onto the post, but Bailey, a £175,000 buy from Birmingham City, was to react the quickest, pouncing on the rebound to complete his hat-trick, tapping the ball home.

It should actually have ended 5-1, as Wegrie spurned an excellent opportunity when he scooped the ball over the bar when ideally placed in front of goal. In any case, it was still United's worst home defeat since 1978.

Strangely enough, Ferguson had warned his players about becoming complacent, but it had apparently fallen on deaf ears. 'Unbelievable' was almost all the United manager could mutter afterwards. 'We were totally outplayed. I have no excuses whatsoever.

'It was a nightmare start to the New Year. We lacked the determination and organisation that has got us where we are.

'Now the players have to prove it was a one-off and I'm sure they will. I'm convinced they will not let me down like that again.

'We were bad right throughout the team and maybe it was a good time to get a performance like that out of their systems.'

13

Middlesbrough (H)

11 March 1992

Many still felt that the title was United's, even more so after defeating rivals Leeds United 3-1 at Elland Road in the League Cup and 1-0, again in Yorkshire, in the FA Cup, but it was not to be. There was, however, success in one of the cup competitions.

In the FA Cup, United became the first side to go out of the competition on penalty kicks, losing 4-2 to Southampton at Old Trafford, but in the League Cup they were to defeat Nottingham Forest 1-0 in the final at Wembley.

That final was as far from a classic encounter as you could probably get, but the home leg of the semi-final against Middlesbrough was to conjure up one of those magical nights under the Old Trafford floodlights that are still talked about today.

United: Schmeichel, Parker, Irwin, Bruce, Webb, Pallister, Robson, Ince, McClair, Sharpe (1), Giggs (1). Substitutes: Phelan and Robins, both not used.
Middlesbrough: Pears, Fleming, Philips, Kernaghan, Mohan, Mustoe, Slaven (1), Pollock, Wilkinson, Hendrie, Ripley. Substitutes: Falconer for Ripley. Proctor not used.
Score: 2-1
Attendance: 45,875

The atmosphere in the early years of Alex Ferguson's tenure was far from inspiring. At times it was vindictive and nasty, with the manager and certain players feeling the brunt of the supporters' frustrations. But, as the song goes, 'what a difference a day makes' – what a difference some silverware makes. With a title challenge ongoing and the chance of a Wembley cup final on the horizon, the Old Trafford faithful were suddenly back to their vibrant best, creating an atmosphere that would make Middlesbrough's visit in the second leg of the Rumbelows Cup semi-final one of those nights to remember.

In the first leg, the Second Division side had held United to a 0-0 draw or, more to the point, Peter Schmeichel had been in a defiant mood. One save in particular, leaping high to his left and clawing away a Falconer header, was enough on its own to ensure that the visitors returned to Manchester in a favourable position to go through to the final.

With the scores level, there was certainly everything to play for, and on their first-leg showing, Middlesbrough looked more than capable of springing a surprise on the night.

But the rain-soaked Old Trafford pitch was going to test the footballing ability of both teams.

United, without the suspended Hughes, had eighteen-year-old Ryan Giggs playing in a more central striking role and Lee Sharpe in the starting line-up for only the second time this season. Attacked from the start, it was Middlesbrough who almost took a surprise lead in the second minute when Wilkinson outstepped Bruce inside the area, his header going inches over.

Play was soon swinging from end to end, with Ripley on the 'Boro left causing the United defence numerous problems. Irwin came closest to opening United's account, latching onto a fisted clearance by Pears and letting fly from the edge of the area.

On the greasy surface, there was little room for error and clear-cut opportunities were few and far between, but on the half-hour, United took the lead. The build-up in itself was quality, moving across the pitch from right to left beginning with Ince and then involving Robson, Giggs and McClair, before Webb passed out wide to Sharpe, who left-footed the ball past Pears for his first goal of the season.

Before United could get a proper foothold on the game, 'Boro were searching for the equaliser. Pollock shot over when Slaven was perhaps in a better scoring position. Wilkinson screamed for a penalty after being charged from behind by Bruce, but the referee waved play on. They had to wait, however, until five minutes into the second half before drawing level. Ripley, perhaps the most dangerous of the visitors' players, skipped down the left, evading Parker's sliding tackle before sending an awkward, tantalising ball skimming across the wet surface. Slaven had little else to do than turn the ball in at the near post.

It was now game on. Middlesbrough had the bit between their teeth and their supporters were in full voice. 'You're supposed to be at home,' they goaded the United fans, as the game hung on a slender thread and the atmosphere increased by the minute.

Irwin came close twice, and then the visitors shunned several opportunities of clinching that place in the final. Schmeichel saved at the feet of Wilkinson then Pallister cleared off the line from Hendrie. Substitute Falconer just failed to reach a Slaven cross.

Sharpe came close when he was sent clear by Irwin, but his left-footed shot was saved by former United 'keeper Pears. Then, right at the death, the usually reliable McClair shot wide from a Robson pass and the tie moved into extra time. Play continued to sway from end to end, Schmeichel once again showing his brilliance with a superb save from Falconer's header before the tie was finally decided in the 106th minute. Webb's cross was headed down by Robson and Giggs shot home with ease.

At the final whistle, many of the supporters, whose magnificent support had added to the atmosphere on the night and inspired United to such a performance, spilled onto the quagmire of a pitch to salute their heroes. It was a support that Alex Ferguson hailed as the 'greatest backing the team has had since I arrived'.

'It was a memorable occasion for the club and one of my greatest nights at Old Trafford – I'll remember it forever.'

14

Sheffield Wednesday (H)

10 April 1993

Despite Leeds United losing 4-1 at Queens Park Rangers, they still managed to maintain their momentum and snatch the title from United's grasp.

A 2-1 defeat at home to Nottingham Forest and, two days later, an embarrassing 1-0 defeat at Upton Park (West Ham United were to finish bottom) in the third last fixture of the season were major blows to their title aspirations.

In the penultimate fixture of the season, United travelled to Liverpool, while Leeds visited Sheffield United, where the Elland Road side ran out winners by the odd goal in seven, an own goal clinching the victory. It was a result United and their supporters knew before they ventured out into the Anfield cauldron. Liverpool took great pleasure in defeating United 2-0, thus handing the title to Leeds.

Alex Ferguson hinted that the main reasons behind the title slump were 'the poor performances after Christmas, the dreadful state of the Old Trafford pitch and the killing climax of playing five games in ten days'.

But perhaps the loss of three points on New Year's Day, in the 4-1 defeat by Queens Park Rangers, was a clear indication that there were still one or two things to iron out before that championship trophy could be decorated once again with red-and-white ribbons.

Eric Cantona was an inspiration to the championship success of Leeds United, but could the enigmatic Frenchman concoct a similar form of magic on the opposite side of the Pennines?

Aston Villa, under former United manager Ron Atkinson, was the major threat in the chase for the 1992/93 championship and an inspired Mark Bosnich display in an absorbing encounter at Old Trafford in mid-March earned Villa a 1-1 draw and kept them level on points with United.

By early April, Villa were in top spot, although having played a game more, with Norwich City second, United two points behind the latter and four behind the Midlanders, but the Carrow Road side had been put firmly in their place when United left East Anglia with a resounding 3-1 victory.

Just a point behind Villa, United were entertaining Sheffield Wednesday at Old Trafford and, as the afternoon unfolded, it was one that was to be crucial in the destination of the 1992/93 championship.

United: Schmeichel, Parker, Irwin, Bruce (2), Sharpe, Pallister, Cantona, Ince, McClair, Hughes, Giggs. Substitutes: Robson for Parker. Phelan not used.
Sheffield Wednesday: Woods, Nilsson, Worthington, Palmer, Sheridan (1), Anderson, Wilson, Waddle, King, Jemson, Watson. Substitute: Bart-Williams for Wilson and Bright for Jemson.
Score: 2-1
Attendance: 40,102

Prior to the match, Alex Ferguson said that the players and supporters should enjoy the match against Sheffield Wednesday: 'We are in a marvellous position as we go neck and neck for the championship and it would be a pity if we all got so full of anxiety and worry that we failed to appreciate our exciting situation or what we are watching, I believe it's something very special.'

Although in fifth place, some fifteen points behind United, Sheffield Wednesday could not be considered as pushovers, an easy three points in the quest for the championship. However, without their two first-choice strikers – Warhurst and Hirst – it was obvious to all that there would be a more defensive display than normal by the Yorkshire side.

With only nine minutes gone, Cantona, playing in a deep-lying role, ran onto an Ince through ball, crossing the ball towards Giggs. But Ince, unaware of the young Welshman's presence and having continued his forward run, lunged at the ball and Woods saved with ease. Two minutes later, McClair was denied by his former teammate Viv Anderson, the defender blocking the shot, and then by Woods, who dived to make a splendid save.

But it wasn't all United. In the twenty-first minute, Irwin had to head away a Waddle cross from underneath the crossbar as Jemson challenged. Most of the action, however, continued to be in the Wednesday half of the pitch. Chris Waddle, on the right, was always a constant source of danger, leaving Parker stranded in a race for the ball and ghosting past Sharpe and Hughes with ease. His presence alone kept the United defence more than occupied.

Despite the ever-dangerous Waddle and United's attacks from all fronts, the first half ended goalless, something that did not concern the home support too much. That concern, however, certainly did surface in the sixty-fourth minute, although the turning point in the game occurred three minutes earlier.

Keeping up with play, referee Michael Peck suddenly pulled up with a leg injury and, after prolonged treatment, he decided that he was unable to continue and was replaced by John Hilditch. Before the 'new' referee had time to settle into the role, Waddle was once again moving into the United penalty area, and on this occasion he was tackled by Ince and went down. Without hesitation, Hilditch pointed to the spot.

An eerie silence fell over Old Trafford as Sheridan, who grew up a mere stone's throw from the ground, placed the ball on the spot. That silence was only broken moments later by the Wednesday support, as the ball flew past Schmeichel to give the visitors the lead.

There was now an urgency about United's play, the radios around the ground informing the faithful that Villa were still being held at home to Coventry, but the minutes were slowly ticking away. The disappointment of the previous season began to resurface amid the bright afternoon sunshine.

It was now one eye on the pitch, the other on the watch. The ninety minutes were now up and it was now a case of how much time would be added on. Villa had drawn 0-0 with Coventry.

Attacking the Stretford End, United won a corner. The Wednesday penalty area was packed with red, and blue-and-white shirts as Irwin's corner floated over. Powering forward through everyone came Steve Bruce, his header looping over a helpless Woods. Old Trafford erupted. 1-1. A point was better than nothing. United were still in with a shout of that elusive title.

But still play continued. Buses and trains were forgotten about. No one was leaving.

United, not content with a point and unconcerned about a Wednesday counter-attack, continued to push forward. It was now six minutes into injury time. Gary Pallister, wide on the right, crossed the ball into the Wednesday area, where it deflected off the head of a blue-and-white-shirted defender. As it dropped from the air, the burly figure of Steve Bruce was once again charging forward and again he powered the ball towards the Wednesday goal. Woods, diving to his left, could do little to prevent it going in. Old Trafford erupted for a second time, threatening the Richter scale.

United were in front. Fergie time was born.

Brian Kidd was on his knees on the pitch. Alex Ferguson was attempting his own celebrations on the touchline. 'Always look on the Bright Side of Life' echoed around the ground.

Finally the whistle went to signal the end of the game. It was also the moment that everyone believed that the twenty-six-year jinx was well and truly over.

Having regained his breath, the United manager said, 'After we won at Norwich a week ago I said that we had to go out and win our remaining matches and that's still the case.

'Now we've got five games left and we've just got to keep winning. We know that if we win them all we'll win the title. Our destiny is in our own hands.'

15

Oldham Athletic (N)

10 April 1994

United were not required to win their remaining five fixtures, although they did anyway, as on the afternoon of 2 May, Aston Villa lost 1-0 at home to Oldham Athletic and the title race was over.

'The players who have won the championship have joined the greats of the past,' said the United manager.

'By winning the League for the first time in twenty-six years they have rid the club of its albatross and opened the door for United to emerge as a force for the future. We suffered pain and agony last season when we led the field only to come to grief at the end. I think maybe you have to suffer first. It can make you stronger and I think we have been.

'We can win the championship for a year or two.'

Having at last banished the haunting spectre of the League championship that had hung over the club for so long, it was now a case of making up for lost time, and as the 1993/94 season moved towards its finale, United were once again at the forefront, ahead of a bankrolled Blackburn Rovers.

While maintaining that championship challenge, they had also kept a healthy interest in the FA Cup. Away victories against Sheffield United (1-0), Norwich City (2-0), and Wimbledon (3-0) took them into the sixth round and the first home tie of the competition against Charlton Athletic, where a 3-1 victory earned a place in the last four. Now Oldham Athletic, as it was in 1990, stood between United and a place in the final.

There was no short journey to Maine Road on this occasion, but with a long haul to Wembley for the semi-final tie and having already lost out to Aston Villa beneath the twin towers a matter of weeks earlier in the League Cup final, Alex Ferguson certainly did not want a similar experience this time around.

United went to London with Cantona, Keane and Kanchelskis all suspended, and although the United manager expected his team to win, he took nothing for granted. 'We are not doing too badly. We set our stall out to win the League and we are right up there leading. We got to one cup final, and hopefully we can get to another.

'So long as we win the League, I don't care if Oldham beat us – they can win 10-0 for all I care!'

United: Schmeichel, Parker, Bruce, Pallister, Irwin, Sharpe, McClair, Ince, Giggs, Hughes (1), Dublin. Substitutes: Butt for Parker and Robson for Dublin. Sealey not used.
Oldham Athletic: Hallworth, Makin, Jobson, Fleming, Pointon (1), Bernard, Milligan, Henry, Holden, Beckford, Sharp. Substitutes: Gerrard, Brennan and Ritchie not used.
Score: 1-1
Attendance: 56,399

Cup semi-finals can be nerve-wracking occasions, as one mere slip can see your dreams come tumbling down. In the season-long League campaign, you can lose two or three games, even more, and still snatch the title. But in the cup, you get one, sometimes two oppositions, but it is basically what you do over that initial ninety minutes that governs the difference between success and failure.

It was the first season of FA Cup semi-finals being dragged to Wembley, nothing more than a money-grabbing decision by the Football Association, but the football lovers from the North still made their way down the M6 in their thousands that Sunday afternoon.

The game, in all honesty, was a far cry from being an excellent advert for the famous old competition. 'A dour, drab semi-final of many fouls and little coherent movement' was how David Lacey of the *Guardian* described the encounter, with Rob Hughes of the *Times* echoing those thoughts, writing, 'The fare had been wretched during the ninety minutes.' He also added, 'How far United have tumbled from their flowing arrogance, their hypnotic flair which for half this season transcended English football. Now, not only do they transgress the laws, not only do they give shameful example to watching schoolboys, but their nerve is tenuous.'

Oldham, perhaps aware that they could not match United for flair, decided that brawn might win them the day, and Milligan ran around like a terrier on the beach, chasing and snapping at everything. Ince carried United for long periods and came close to scoring in the sixteenth minute, his header just going wide of the post. His volley, which dipped narrowly over the crossbar just before the interval, was only the second time that United had threatened Hallworth in the Oldham goal.

The Boundary Park side, 5-1 outsiders to win the tie, denied United any space or time on the ball and should have gone in front when Holden cut the ball to Sharp, who left-footed the ball wide from 12 yards out. Indeed, the Latics front man should have won the game on his own with a hat-trick, as he was denied by Schmeichel in the fifty-third minute, the Dane saving well from a snap shot at the near post and again later on when, unmarked, he fired a Holden free-kick into the side netting.

On the United flanks, both Giggs and Sharpe were subdued and it was only toward the closing stages of the ninety minutes that the former began to show anything like his true form. Irwin tested Hallworth with a free-kick in the seventy-fourth minute, but it was Oldham who grew in stature as the game wore on.

With no goals in the ninety minutes of normal play, it was into extra time, the paying public at least getting an additional half-hour for their outlay – something in the way of compensation for the lack of entertainment they had endured.

The game became more ragged than before, with Pointon, Henry, Ince and Hughes all going into the referee's notebook in quick succession. But it was Hughes who came close to breaking the deadlock midway through the additional thirty minutes when, although closely marked by Fleming, he met Irwin's cross with his head, but could only watch as Hallworth turned the ball over the bar.

But a minute into the second period of extra time, the tide suddenly turned. Makin forced a corner and, as Holden swung the ball over, Schmeichel came off his line. However, in his fumbled attempt to catch the ball, he collided with Steve Bruce and the ball broke free, going as far as Pointon, who left-footed the ball through a forest of legs and into the United net.

Ferguson replaced Parker with Butt in an effort to push United forward with fresh legs, but the game was slowly slipping away from United, while the Oldham bench sensed victory was theirs. With only forty-nine seconds remaining, few would have argued.

United booted the ball forward in hope; Oldham cleared it anywhere. Forward came United again and a half clearance saw McClair, with his back to goal, kicked the ball over his head into the Oldham area with no idea where it might land. As it dropped, Mark Hughes, sandwiched between two defenders, stuck out his right leg and connected with the ball, propelling it beyond the reach of Hallworth to earn United a replay.

'It was going to need a stroke of genius to get United out of it at that stage and that's what happened,' said Oldham manager Joe Royle. 'Hughes made the volley with the ball dropping over his shoulder. With anyone else it would probably have gone over the stand.'

'When you're a goal down with less than a minute left you need a miracle, and that's exactly what we got,' admitted Alex Ferguson.

'You never give up at Manchester United, but I thought it was going away from us until Sparky struck.'

16

Port Vale (A)

21 September 1994

In the Maine Road replay, it was a different Manchester United and one that Oldham could not handle. Goals from Irwin, Kanchelskis, Robson and Giggs brushed the Latics aside, with Pointon's goal, which gave his team hope at 2-1, being little more than a consolation.

In the Wembley final, Chelsea fared no better than Oldham, conceding four without reply as United swept to the League and cup double, having overcome Blackburn's challenge in the League to clinch the title by eight points. But despite the double success, Alex Ferguson was not content to rest on his laurels and had one eye on the future.

Few beyond those who followed United's reserve and junior sides knew what lay away from the glare of first-team football, what precocious talents were learning their trade as professional footballers. Such was the talent outwith the first-team ranks that Alex Ferguson did not have to think twice when deciding to throw them into the fray of a League Cup tie, a competition that mattered little when there were greater prizes to be won at home and abroad.

Port Vale: Musslewhite, Sandeman (1), Griffiths, D. Glover, Tankard, van der Laan, Porter, Kent, Naylor, J. Glover, Foyle. Substitutes: Burke for Naylor. Walker and van Heusden not used.
United: Walsh, G. Neville, May, Keane, Irwin, Gillespie, Butt, Beckham, Davies, McClair, Scholes (2). Substitutes: O'Kane for Neville and Sharpe for Butt. Pilkington not used.
Score: 2-1
Attendance: 18,605

With a crucial European Cup tie against Galatasaray in Istanbul on the horizon, now was as good a time as any to inject his preferred starting line-up with some non-first-team individuals, resting his regulars for the more testing ninety minutes that lay ahead.

United's visit to Port Vale for the Coca-Cola second-round tie had sold out within twenty-four hours of the 22,000 tickets going on sale. But little did the locals know that their admission money would not earn them the right to see the likes of Hughes,

Cantona, Schmeichel and Giggs. The manager was undaunted by the threat of a £50,000 Football League fine for fielding a supposedly understrength team.

The announcement in the national press that Ferguson was intent on sending out an understrength team did not go down too well in the Potteries, with Stoke-on-Trent North MP Joan Walley going as far as to complain that the 17,000 Vale supporters who paid to see the second-round first-leg clash 'deserved better'. Even the trading standards authorities got their tuppenceworth in.

With Ferguson's selection in mind, it was an ideal opportunity for the home side to gain a first-leg advantage that could possibly see them progress in the competition, but they were to find that even an understrength Manchester United, containing some nondescript individuals, was difficult to beat.

Containing a quintet of nineteen-year-olds and only four internationals, and under the guidance of Brian McClair, it was certainly an unfamiliar United side. Alex Ferguson's decision was looking to have backfired when Port Vale took the lead in the seventh minute. Kent's corner was headed out by debutant Paul Scholes, but only as far as Sandeman, whose 25-yard shot flew past Gary Walsh via an ever-so-slight touch from the head of Glover.

Beckham, another debutant, and Butt in the United midfield, sprayed the ball around with style, frequently supplying Davies and Gillespie, another making his initial appearance on the flanks, but did little in the way of stretching the home defence. Their failure to do so almost proved costly when Port Vale nearly doubled their advantage in the eighteenth minute. Walsh was drawn out of his area as Foyle chased a through ball, but the 'keeper's clearance went only as far as Glover. In his haste to catch Walsh out of his goal, the Vale front man rushed his shot and it rolled wide.

Had Glover scored, then the course of the tie might have changed completely, but the miss was to allow United into the game nine minutes prior to the interval. An under-hit pass by Tankard was snatched upon by Scholes and the ginger-haired youngster drew Musselwhite from his goal before chipping the ball in off the far post. The home side thought they had regained the lead when Sandeman forced the ball home after Walsh had fumbled a shot from Porter, but a linesman flag for offside denied them the goal.

Nine minutes into the second half, United took the lead. Simon Davies mesmerised Griffiths before crossing towards the near post, where Scholes nipped in front of his marker to nod the ball home. '2-1 to the youth team' and 'They're going to school in the morning' taunted the travelling United support.

Irwin was booked for a foul on Naylor, probably more for being a City supporter than for causing any danger, as Port Vale pushed forward in an effort to save face and, in something of a rare attack, van der Laan fired over in the sixty-seventh minute.

As the game wore on, United's confidence grew, as they teased and tormented their hosts, their lack of experience far from obvious and the Port Vale fans, although denied the presence of a few international stars, were certainly not short-changed. The quality of football was far superior to what they were normally used to, while they could also say they were present at the start of something big.

'The young players showed no fear,' said a jubilant United manager after the game. 'They got hold of the ball and passed it around in great style.

'They got the goals at the right time too, because they tired towards the end, which was only to be expected.

'Paul Scholes took his goals superbly and the team won well. I have talked for two years about these boys and they had to be played. If I hadn't, people would have started to ask what I was on about.

'We have got to give them the chance to realise their potential and this was a start for them. It was good for the fans to see them at this level too.'

17

Crystal Palace (A)

25 January 1995

The Red Devils. On occasion, the nickname was more than apt. Despite the brilliance that the various individuals who pulled on the famous red shirt possessed, there were occasions when the red mist would descend and the shine would suddenly become tarnished.

More often than not, the actions of the guilty came from provocation. Such was the case on the evening of Wednesday 25 January 1995: a night that was to test Alex Ferguson's managerial capabilities to the full.

Crystal Palace: Martyn, Patterson, Shaw, Coleman, Gordon, Southgate (1), Pitcher, Newman, Salako, Dowie, Armstrong. Substitutes: Preece for Dowie. Bowry and Wilmot not used.
United: Schmeichel, Keane, May (1), Pallister, Irwin, Giggs, McClair, Ince, Sharpe, Cantona, Cole. Substitutes: Kanchelskis for Sharpe. Scholes and Walsh not used.
Score: 1-1
Attendance: 18,224

With only one victory in their previous eleven Premier League fixtures, the odds were stacked against Crystal Palace pulling off a shock victory. United, on the other hand, were unbeaten in seven, but the south London club were undaunted by their opponents and their speed and determination caused United numerous problems.

May, playing in place of the suspended Bruce, often struggled, but Palace failed to capitalise on any opportunities they created, showing a nervousness in front of goal, with their failure in front of the United goal often leading to counter-attacks from the visitors. In dealing with those United attacks, Palace relied constantly on playing an offside game, although at times it was something of a gamble.

Cole sent McClair through in the eleventh minute, but Martyn was alert to the danger, smothering the ball before the Scot could reach it. The United frontman, however, was more frustrated by the service he was receiving from teammates, and the high balls that were floated towards him were easily cut out by the tall figure of Coleman.

A couple of hard tackles seemed to ruffle Cantona, and the Frenchman drifted out of the game, with his first touch being far from the normal. Salako, on the left, caused United problems, with Keane booked for stopping the winger in a rather uncompromising way. Then, shortly before the break, Armstrong tested Schmeichel with a powerful shot on the turn, which the 'keeper did well to hold.

Armstrong had also seen a header skim the United crossbar in the thirty-eighth minute, one of only two real scoring opportunities in the opening forty-five minutes. Salako had the other on the stroke of half-time, but from a poor punched clearance by Schmeichel, he shot wide of the United goal.

As the second half got underway, United began to show something of an improvement, but with only three minutes gone, Cantona awoke from his slumber. A challenge by Shaw was certainly not to his liking and, as the pair once again challenged for the ball moments later, the Frenchman aimed a kick at the Palace player.

Almost immediately, referee Alan Wilkie produced the red card and sent Cantona off for what was the fifth time in his Manchester United career. Accepting his fate, Cantona walked from the pitch, but as he reached the touchline, he suddenly, and at the time unexplainably, launched himself off the ground and into the crowd, making contact with a male supporter, exchanging a number of punches before police, stewards, players and backroom staff moved in to separate the pair.

Cantona was led off down the touchline to the dressing rooms.

Alex Ferguson was rather oblivious as to what had just taken place a few yards along the touchline. 'I only saw the aftermath, a punch being thrown,' he was later to admit. 'Then I saw Eric lying over a hoarding and I thought maybe he'd been dragged into the crowd or something. I didn't fully understand how serious it was that night, even having spoken to the police.'

It wasn't until he got home, and already having ignored his son's suggestion to watch the video highlights, that he rose in the early hours, unable to sleep, and the full impact of the incident hit home. 'It was terrible. I couldn't believe it. How could Eric have done it?'

The incident stunned players and spectators alike, but within minutes, United had regained their composure and taken the lead. David May headed home his first League goal for the club from Sharpe's centre. United held the lead until the seventieth minute, when a Southgate snapshot, amid a goalmouth scramble, secured a point for the home side.

The result, other than a dropped point for United, was totally insignificant. Indeed, for many, following Cantona's dismissal, the remainder of the game passed in a blur, with the match reports in the following day's newspapers confined to a mere couple of paragraphs. Cantona, however, was front-page news.

'You Thug', proclaimed the *Sun*, while the *Express* went with 'The Shame of Cantona'. Even the *Scottish Daily Record* went with 'Cantonargh'.

United issued the player with a ban for the remainder of the season and a £20,000 fine, while the Football Association stepped in, much to United's disgust and displeasure, with their own eight-month ban and a further £10,000 fine. An appearance in court saw the Frenchman given a two-week prison sentence, but this was overturned on appeal to 120 hours' community service.

Cantona's actions at Selhurst Park were also to cost United the League and cup double.

18

Ipswich Town (H)

4 March 1995

Goals were not exactly 'ten a penny', so to speak, during the first half of the 1994/95 season, although everyone rejoiced in the five that had been put past City in November. Wrexham had also conceded five, but few would have expected anything different against lesser opposition.

Cantona and Kanchelskis were the club's leading scorers with fourteen each, but on a match-by-match basis, a couple of goals could be seen as average.

Ipswich Town had conceded sixty in their thirty Premiership fixtures and were second bottom with a mere twenty-three points, forty behind United, so could the Old Trafford regulars expect a few more goals than they were normally treated to when Ipswich headed north?

United: Schmeichel, Keane (1), Irwin, Bruce, Pallister, Ince (1), McClair, Kanchelskis, Cole (4), Hughes (2), Giggs. Substitutes: Sharpe for Keane and Butt for Bruce. Walsh not used.
Ipswich Town: Forrest, Yallop (1 own goal), Thompson, Wark, Linighan, Palmer, Williams, Sedgley, Slater, Mathie, Chapman. Substitutes: Marshall for Chapman. Mason and Morgan not used.
Score: 9-0
Attendance: 43,804

On their two previous visits, Ipswich had left Old Trafford with draws due to their defensive displays, but prior to their latest journey to Manchester, manager George Burley insisted his side would be a bit more adventurous. Wrong move.

In the opposite dugout, Alex Ferguson had resisted the temptation to leave out 'want-away' winger Kanchelskis, playing him up front alongside his new forward pairing of Hughes and Cole, as United challenged Blackburn Rovers at the top of the table with three points separating the two teams. Right move.

Ipswich, despite their lowly position, had won at Liverpool, drawn at Newcastle and beaten United 3-2 at Portman Road, but they were to find themselves a goal behind after a quarter of an hour, and from then on were not so much chasing the game as trying to keep the scoreline respectable.

United swept forward from the kick-off, winning two corners in the opening couple of minutes. Andy Cole, guilty of missing a couple of good scoring opportunities in the previous week's 1-0 defeat at Everton, again frustrated the United support. On one occasion he stood on the ball instead of kicking it, much to the delight of the small travelling support who voiced their opinion of his £7-million price tag.

Hughes, clearly not wanting to be outshone by Cole, fought for every ball in all areas of the pitch and was instrumental in United's opening goal in the fifteenth minute. Irwin moved forward from defence unchallenged, finding Hughes, who moved the ball across the edge of the Ipswich area where Keane, unmarked, diverted the ball wide off the reach of Forrest in the Ipswich goal.

Within nine minutes it was 2-0. Giggs charged down an attempted clearance by Yallop and, as the ball bobbled down the touchline, the young Welshman ran after it and crossed into the Ipswich area, where Cole knocked it home.

It was game over in the thirty-sixth minute, when Cole added his second to make it 3-0, Kanchelskis crossing and an overhead kick from Hughes crashing against the crossbar, the ball falling conveniently for Cole to score.

Ipswich, to their credit, did attack as their manager had promised, winning two corners prior to United's third, while Mathie shot weakly from only 8 yards out, allowing the United defence to clear.

With Sharpe on for Keane at the start of the second half, United had more attacking options and it was not long before the visitors were on the back foot and the scoreboard was going into overdrive. Wark managed to rob Cole as the United man was about to shoot, but he could do little as United scored their fourth, fifth and sixth goals in a six-minute, early second-half spell.

The stadium announcer gave the fourth to Cole, but it was more of a Yallop own goal from an Irwin centre than the United man's hat-trick. Hughes claimed the fifth, scoring at the far post, via the underside of the crossbar, from a Giggs corner, with the Welshman also claiming the sixth, heading home a blocked Giggs shot.

Ipswich frantically tried to keep United out, but they had no answer to their attacking play from every area of the pitch.

Cole eventually did claim his hat-trick in the sixty-fifth minute. With Hughes feeding McClair and Forrest unable to keep hold of the ball, Cole nipped in to beat Forrest yet again.

How many more could United score?

A Premier League record was set with the eighth and it was one that illustrated just how much disarray Ipswich were in. Forrest handled the ball outside his area and technically should have been sent off, but the 'keeper was punished more than the yellow card he was shown, as before he could get back to his goal, Ince had taken the kick, chipping it into the vacant net.

Three minutes from time, Cole claimed his fourth and United's ninth, turning quickly to shoot home from 6 yards, to give United their biggest victory since the 10-1 defeat of Wolves 103 years previously in October 1882.

'That was the biggest victory I have ever had as a manager,' declared a delighted Alex Ferguson. 'When I was manager of Aberdeen I had 8-0 wins over Motherwell and Meadowbank, but this was the best of the lot. Everybody out there was magnificent. It was a once-in-a-lifetime display, a day when everybody was on top of his job. A marvellous performance and the way we played supersedes the goals we scored. The movement and passing and the passion of our play was terrific all through the game.'

19

West Ham United (A)

14 May 1995

It was a war of nerves at the top of the Premiership table on the final day of the 1994/95 season.

A victory for United at Upton Park against West Ham United and a draw or a defeat for Blackburn Rovers at Anfield would see the championship trophy head towards Old Trafford.

United were indeed on course for the League and cup double, as they had a Wembley date with Everton the following Saturday. But everything was far from straightforward.

Blackburn were managed by Liverpool old boy Kenny Dalglish, so the odds were already heavily stacked against United. This was even without taking into consideration that West Ham, three years previously and already doomed to relegation, had defeated United 1-0 and virtually handed the championship to Leeds.

At the end of the day, United simply had to win and let fate decide.

West Ham United: Miklosko, Breacker, Rieper, Potts, Rowland, Hughes (1), Bishop, Moncur, Holmes, Hutchison, Morley. Substitutes: Allen for Hutchison and Webster for Hughes. Sealey not used.
United: Schmeichel, G. Neville, Bruce, Pallister, Irwin, Butt, Keane, McClair (1), Ince, Sharpe, Cole. Subsitutes: Hughes for Butt and Scholes for Keane. Walsh not used.
Score: 1-1
Attendance: 24,783

It was rather ironic that United should set a new Premiership record when they put nine past a hapless Ipswich Town, yet failed to win the championship because they could not score one solitary goal against West Ham United.

When it had come down to a matter of needing a victory to perhaps clinch the title, Alex Ferguson made a strange decision in leaving Mark Hughes on the bench, not giving him a taste of the action until after the interval.

It was something of a nervous start by United, who breathed a sigh of relief in the twenty-third minute when Holmes struck the bar, but they were to go behind on the half-hour, when an accurate cross from Holmes was met perfectly by Michael Hughes, who side-footed on the volley past a hapless Schmeichel. Seven minutes later,

United should have drawn level, but Cole could only watch in anguish as his effort struck the foot of the post.

It wasn't until the introduction of Hughes that United came alive. One early pass sent Keane down the wing, the Irishman's cross being met by Sharpe, but his header was brilliantly saved by Miklosoko.

In the fifty-second minute, a foul on Cole gave United a free-kick and, from Neville's floated ball, McClair, at the near post, headed home the equaliser. Blackburn had already taken the lead at Anfield, so there was still work to be done.

Eleven minutes later, news filtered through that Liverpool had equalised and the game suddenly took on a new meaning. United upped a gear in search of a winner that could mean so much.

Irwin drove a free-kick just over, then Miklosoko again pulled off an excellent save when Hughes looked likely to score with a header from a Pallister back-header. The Hammers then had a couple of chances, but play was mainly around the home goal.

As the game wore on, it looked as though the title could be snatched from the hands of Blackburn Rovers as, unlike Wimbledon, the ball did not fly from one end to the other, but seemed to be tied to the West Ham goalpost on a piece of elastic as it bobbled and bounced around the area.

Ten minutes remained and twice Andy Cole was set up with the type of opportunity that he should have put away blindfolded. But twice, the United forward failed to beat the West Ham goalkeeper.

Suddenly the transistor radios on the Upton Park terracing informed the United support that Liverpool were in front. Play became even more frantic around the Hammers' goalmouth, but time was running out.

Two minutes to play and Scholes set up Cole, but the opportunity passed, as did another in injury time.

Transistors were also to the fore at Anfield, and the whole stadium erupted into a wall of noise as the news filtered through that United had failed to score the goal that would have won them the title. The Liverpool support could not have been happier had their own team lifted the championship.

It was a forlorn United side who slowly trudged off the Upton Park pitch.

Many pointed the finger at the United manager for his team's failure, citing his decision to leave Hughes out of his starting line-up as being a major factor. 'We had to take the wind out of West Ham's sails in the first half and I explained to Mark that he was always going to come on,' responded Ferguson. 'We have done well in the past with only one up front. It was the right decision.'

He added, 'My players were marvellous. It was a fantastic performance but it just did not go our way. We did more than we needed to win the game but maybe fate was against us. Still, it has been a tremendous effort this season considering all the cautions, all the injuries, all the suspensions, everything that has gone against us.'

The failure to overcome West Ham had something of a knock-on effect, as the following weekend United returned to London, a few miles further north on this occasion, to face Everton at Wembley in the FA Cup final. Once again, their failure to find the back of the net proved fatal, as they lost to the only goal of the game.

20

Aston Villa (A)

19 August 1995

Everyone wants to get out of the starting blocks with a burst of speed, edging ahead of their rivals from the outset, hoping that they can maintain that momentum over the course of the season-long race. But for United, following a summer of discontent among the rank-and-file support, with a poll showing that 57 per cent of the United supporters wanted rid of manager Alex Ferguson following the disappointment of winning nothing during the previous campaign and the manager's decision to sell Mark Hughes and Paul Ince, along with the impeding transfer of Andrei Kanchelskis, it was to be the worst possible start to the new campaign.

Aston Villa: Bosnich, Charles, Wright, Southgate, McGrath, Ehiogu, Taylor (1), Draper (1), Milosevic, Yorke (1 pen.), Townsend. Substitutes: Johnson for Milosevic and Scimeca for Yorke. Spink not used.
United: Schmeichel, Parker, Irwin, Keane Sharpe, Pallister, Butt, G. Neville, McClair, Scholes, P. Neville. Substitutes: Beckham (1) for P. Neville and O'Kane for Pallister. Davies not used.
Score: 3-1
Attendance: 34,655

There were no new signings in the United line-up for the opening-day fixture against Aston Villa, Alex Ferguson keeping his wallet firmly shut during the close season, although there were certainly changes in personnel from the team that had lost to Everton in the FA Cup final back in May.

Into the starting line-up came Phil Neville and Paul Scholes, with David Beckham, Simon Davies and John O'Kane on the bench, giving the United line-up something of a youthful look. The equally fresh-faced Gary Neville and Nicky Butt were also included in Alex Ferguson's opening-day XI, with seven of the fourteen players on duty under twenty-one years of age and all having progressed through the youth team. It was something of a gamble by the United manager, and in hindsight, one that was to pay great dividends, but on that sunny afternoon in the Midlands, many were to question his judgement.

'United crash at first hurdle', 'Villa expose youth policy', 'Ferget It United – Alex kids are given a canning', 'United kids fail to grow up in time', 'United hope grey day is a hiccup' and 'United faithful display frustration' were just a few of the headlines that followed United's 3-1 humiliation.

United were to find themselves a goal behind after only fourteen minutes. A through ball from Townsend to Yorke saw the Villa forward cross into the United goalmouth, where a deflection enabled Charles to pick out Taylor, who had little problem in finding the net from 6 yards out.

It was 2-0 thirteen minutes later, with the United defence once again found wanting. Phil Neville was dispossessed by Wright and the ball moved quickly between Draper, Yorke and Milosevic, before the former moved unchallenged into space before beating Schmeichel with ease.

United did display some neat touches, but without the penetration of Ince and someone like Hughes to lead the attack, they failed to make much headway against a Villa team who were now full of confidence and, in the thirty-seventh minute, one that was holding a 3-0 lead. Draper sent a long pass towards Milosevic, but as the Villa forward moved in on goal, he looked as though he had overrun the ball, and was sent tumbling rather theatrically by Schmeichel's somewhat careless intervention. Yorke made no mistake from the penalty spot.

Despite passing the ball about well, the visitors had only looked like scoring on one occasion, when Ehiogu miskicked a Scholes pass in the twenty-fifth minute, leaving Butt with a clear run on goal from midfield, but his shot was rushed and flew high and wide.

In those opening forty-five minutes, Villa had looked a completely different side to the one that had narrowly escaped relegation only a couple of months previously, and during the interval the United support could only hope that the second half would not be a repeat of the first.

As those second forty-five minutes got underway, United were seen to have reverted back to a 4-4-2 formation – Beckham replacing Phil Neville – having begun the game with a more cautious five-man defence. Had they managed to pull a goal back early on, the game might have taken on a completely different look.

Although they were to dominate the second period as much as Villa had the first, they lacked a killer instinct and were not helped when Pallister had to leave the field with an injury in the fifty-ninth minute. But they continued to press forward to the best of their ability and it was only the form of Bosnich in the Villa goal that prevented them from scoring on several occasions. One stunning save saw the Australian palm the ball over the bar from a Keane header, following good work from Neville and Scholes. Another saw a curling shot from McClair also tipped over the bar.

Try as they did, it was not until six minutes from time that United finally managed to beat Bosnich, Beckham scoring from 25 yards, partly aided by a deflection off Southgate.

'I told the youngsters during the interval just to remember they were wearing Manchester United jerseys and they went out to play with confidence, got better and better and dominated the game,' said the United manager after the game. 'But sadly three goals were just too much to find.'

The manager, despite the defeat, was far from disconsolate and went on to add, 'Once we went back to our normal style of play after half-time the players responded very well. Had we scored earlier than Beckham's shot in the eighty-fourth minute it might have been an interesting finish to the match but Bosnich made three or four outstanding saves.'

United's second-half recovery might have given the United manager hope for the future, but on *Match of the Day* that evening, Alan Hansen was far from convinced. Albeit blinkered by his association with a certain Merseyside club, the television pundit proclaimed that 'you do not win championships with kids', a quote that was to launch a thousand t-shirts, while going on to add that Ferguson should go out and buy players and that Liverpool would claim the championship.

He would be made to eat his words many times in the weeks, months and years ahead.

21

Southampton (A)

13 April 1996

A solitary-goal victory against Coventry City at Old Trafford was overshadowed by the horrific injury to David Busst, but the three points were enough to keep United six points clear at the top with only four games remaining. The trip to Southampton the following Saturday, where another three points were expected, would turn out to be no ordinary League fixture.

In years gone by, if United did not play in their traditional red shirt, then they would simply change to white. End of story. But suddenly, there was money to be made from flogging replica shirts, so they changed designs and even colours with an alarming frequency, even adding a third kit to the wardrobe, with some of those actual colour designs being utterly stupid. For some unknown reason, United decided that a grey shirt would look nice as that second change kit. It was a decision that was to prove both fatal and costly. Although the £80-million deal with Umbro was certainly not to be sniffed at...

Southampton: Beasant, Dodd, Benali, Magilton, Neilson, Monkou (1), Le Tissier (1), Venison, Shipperley (1), Charlton, Heaney. Substitutes: Bennett, Widdrington, Waiters – all not used.
United: Schmeichel, Irwin, Bruce, G. Neville, Sharpe, Beckham, Keane, Butt, Giggs (1), Cantona. Substitutes: May for Sharpe and Scholes for Butt. Coton not used.
Score: 3-1
Attendance: 15,262

United's title hopes took a severe knock against relegation strugglers Southampton, and straight from the kick-off they were to find themselves in trouble, Neville hesitating and allowing the ball to fall to Le Tissier who, much to the full-back's relief, hesitated and the opportunity was lost.

Roy Keane made a mess of a back pass, with Gary Neville caught in two minds, and the ball rolled to Jason Dodd, but he was to see his shot blocked by Schmeichel. Unperturbed, United responded with Cole slipping the ball through to Butt, but the midfielder was to fire over.

United, however, had not wrestled the momentum away from the home side, as they were to go a goal behind in the eleventh minute. Bruce pushed Charlton to the ground and, from Le Tissier's free-kick, Monkou headed towards goal. Schmeichel did well to parry the ball, but Monkou latched onto the rebound to score.

With United having won fifteen of their last sixteen fixtures, a fightback was expected, but Southampton continued to press forward. With Dodd shooting wide, Benali was inches away from scoring and then Le Tissier hit the ball past the United 'keeper only to see his effort hit the post.

The visitors' luck ran out in the twenty-third minute when Giggs, caught in possession, was robbed of the ball and Neilson's cross was met by Shipperley, who side-footed home from about 12 yards out. Then, with three minutes remaining before the interval, Southampton scored a third in what was a truly horrendous first half for the visitors.

Dodd crossed from the right and Schmeichel did little more than fumble the ball, which dropped at the feet of Le Tissier. Keeping his cool, the tall striker flicked the ball over the fallen United 'keeper before calmly side-footing the ball home.

Half-time changes are certainly not unusual if the game is not going in your favour, but when it is not a player who is replaced, but your shirt, then there is something definitely wrong.

Having begun the game in their dreary and dull second-choice grey shirt (no doubt having agreed to wear it a certain number of times during the season), although it did suit their play, it came as a surprise all round when United returned to the fray in their third choice blue-and-white stripes. Although why they had both sets of strips with them in the first place is anyone's guess.

If the manager was hoping for a change of luck as well, he was to be disappointed, as the home side could have increased their lead on a couple of occasions. Cantona was surprisingly ineffective, a frustrated Beckham and Keane were booked and it wasn't until three minutes from time that the change of shirt made any difference to the scoreline, when Giggs scored from close range; both Scholes and Beckham having shunned earlier opportunities.

It was an abysmal performance, one that might well have had dire consequences for United, but fortunately it seemed to have the exact opposite effect, galvanising them into a charge to the finishing line and winning their remaining three fixtures without conceding a goal. They beat Leeds 1-0 and Forest 5-0, both at home, and Middlesbrough away 3-0, to win the title by four points from Newcastle. Liverpool were also beaten 1-0 at Wembley in the FA Cup final, to clinch the League and cup double for the second time.

As for the defeat at the Dell, United had never won in the grey strip and it was no secret that neither manager nor players had any real liking for it. After the game, Alex Ferguson had little to say on the matter other than, 'The players said that they couldn't pick each other out wearing the grey shirts.'

Of the game itself, 'It was a nightmare forty-five minutes. We defended badly. It was a poor performance in the first half and at the end of the day we were well beaten, no complaints.'

As for the grey shirts, within forty-eight hours of them being thrown onto the dressing floor at Southampton, it was announced that it had been dropped as the second-choice shirt. A United statement read, 'It has become increasingly apparent that the players have found it difficult to identify each other due to the kit's colour.

'Both Manchester United and Umbro wanted to react to this issue and have decided that, as from the end of the season, the club will no longer wear the grey kit.

'This is a decision made after taking the recent problems into account and after lengthy discussions between the two parties since Saturday. For the 1996/97 season we will register a white shirt as our change jersey, worn with the home shorts and a change white sock.'

22

Southampton (A)

26 October 1996

The 1996/97 season had begun with five wins and four draws in the opening nine League fixtures, but a 5-0 drubbing at St James Park, Newcastle, came as something of a reality check. A visit to Southampton, who were sitting in the lower half of the table, was, on paper, an ideal fixture in which to get back onto a firm footing.

Southampton: Beasant, van Gobbel, Lundekvam, Dryden, Oakley, Neilson, Charlton, Dodd, Le Tissier (1), Berkovic (2), Ostenstad (3). Substitutes: Potter for Charlton, Watson for Le Tissier and Magilton for Neilson. Moss and Slater not used.
United: Schmeichel, G. Neville, May (1), Pallister, P. Neville, Beckham (1), Keane, Butt, Scholes (1), Cantona, Cruyff. Substitutes: Irwin for Pallister, McClair for Butt and Solskjaer for Cruyff. Poborsky and Thornley not used.
Score: 6-3
Attendance: 15,253

At Newcastle, many felt that United had looked tired before they even kicked off, having arrived back in England from Turkey at 4.00 a.m. on the Thursday morning, but you still have to be poor to concede five goals. On the South Coast, United's defence was to go one better.

Last season they'd had the grey shirts to blame for their 3-1 defeat, but today, in what was their heaviest defeat for sixteen years, they had no one to blame but themselves and, in all honesty, they were indeed fortunate just to concede six!

That Cantona failed to control, never mind score, from a Cruyff flick in the second minute was a hint of what was to follow from United. Butt was also unable to find the net from yet another Cruyff flick, although some referees may well have awarded a penalty for the rather cumbersome challenge from Beasant in the Southampton goal. Enraged by the referee's decision, several United players surrounded the official, with Roy Keane's vitriol just a little too prolonged for Jeff Winter's liking, and the United midfielder was booked.

United found themselves a goal behind after only six minutes, Berkovic slamming home after Schmeichel had only managed to parry Ostenstadt's effort.

A couple of offside decisions – one against Scholes which was a definite 'wrong call' – did little to pacify the visitors, and they were to find themselves a man less in the twenty-second minute when Keane, who had already been booked for his show of verbal petulance, was sent off by Jeff Winter for lunging into the back of Lundekvam.

The home side made the most of their advantage, increasing their lead ten minutes before the interval when Le Tissier slipped past both May and Pallister before lobbing the ball over the head of a stranded Schmeichel.

United were perhaps more than a little fortunate to go in at the interval with ten men, as fingers were pointed at Cantona, with claims that on the stroke of half-time, he had kicked and punched Southampton defender van Gobbel as the two players tussled for the ball. The Frenchman had then rolled around under the nose of the referee as if he had been the one attacked.

The half-time pep talk seemed to enliven United. Seven minutes into the second period, Cruyff should certainly have done better from 3 yards out and, had he done so, David May's back-post header from Beckham's free-kick would certainly have put United right back into the game. But it was not to be and the energy that was exerted into those opening minutes soon evaporated. Without Keane, much more was expected from Cantona, but there was nothing in the way of inspiration from the Frenchman. Before long, the home side were once again controlling the play.

The intensity of the first half was certainly not matched in the second, certainly not until the final six minutes when Southampton suddenly regained their enthusiasm and scored a further three goals.

Berkovic made it 4-2 in the eighty-fourth minute, volleying home from just outside the United penalty area. Then, five minutes later, Ostenstad added a fifth, pushing the ball past an advancing Schmeichel.

The big Norwegian claimed his hat-trick four minutes into stoppage time, with Gary Neville, whose final touch sent the ball over the line, more than happy to give the Southampton player the goal. In between Southampton's last two goals, Paul Scholes scored a third for United, flicking the ball home from close range.

It was far from an ideal tenth anniversary present for Alex Ferguson. 'What can you say,' muttered the United manager after the match. 'It was one of those days when everything they hit seemed to go into the back of the net. They played some adventurous and inventive football.

'I thought we were really marvellous in the second half, but we just ran out of steam in the last fifteen minutes.'

23

Chelsea (A)

4 January 1998

In the draw for the third round of the FA Cup, you would always like to be drawn against one of the teams from the lower divisions, preferably at home, but when the balls were pulled out of the velvet bag for that particular round in the 1998 competition, Arsenal were paired with Port Vale, Bradford City travelled to Manchester City and West Ham United took on non-League Emley. United? They had no such luck and were given a trip to Stamford Bridge to face cup holders Chelsea.

The Londoners were a far cry from the side they are today but, managed by Ruud Gullit, they still had one or two notable players in Di Matteo, Zola and Vialli. However, failure to carve out a victory against Southampton, when United had slipped up at Coventry, had seen them slip out of the championship race.

This was all the more reason for their determination in retaining the FA Cup.

Chelsea: De Goey, Clarke, Duberry, Leboeuf, Le Saux (1), Petrescu, Di Matteo, M. Hughes, Nicholls, Zola, Flo. Substitutes: Myers for Nicholls and Vialli (2) for Flo. Hitchcock, Lamburde and P. Hughes not used.
United: Schmeichel, G. Neville, Johnsen, Pallister, Irwin, Beckham (2), Scholes, Butt, Giggs, Cole (2), Sheringham (1). Substitutes: Solskjaer for Scholes. Pilkington, Berg, Clegg and McClair not used.
Score: 5-3
Attendance: 34,792

Ruud Gullit had somewhat transformed Chelsea, building them into formidable opponents, with Alex Ferguson more than a little wary of what lay in front of his team on their journey south. However, as it turned out, he had little to concern himself about, as although it had taken Chelsea twenty-seven years to win the FA Cup, it took them a mere twenty-seven minutes to relinquish their hold on it.

With Dennis Wise suspended, Gullit played former United hero Mark Hughes in midfield, but he was simply making up the numbers as United went about their task in a manner that had many hinting that there was a possibility of Ferguson's team ending the season with a treble celebration.

Twice in the opening five minutes United threatened to take the lead through the artistry of Ryan Giggs who, having evaded a lunging challenge by Petrescu with barely 120 seconds on the clock, threatened Chelsea at every opportunity. From one of his corners, Petrescu headed Johnsen's header off the line, then he opened up the home defence for Cole, his shot bringing out a good save from de Goey. Scholes, prompted by Sheringham, put a shot wide before United took the lead in the twenty-third minute through Beckham.

Andy Cole, in notable form as the Premiership's top scorer with nineteen goals, rounded Leboeuf but found his route to goal blocked, so chipped the ball towards Sheringham, his back header falling to Beckham, who tapped home the opener. Six minutes later, United were two up; Nicholls brought down Giggs and from the free-kick, Beckham's right foot curling the ball round the defensive wall and past the flailing arms of de Goey.

Chelsea had offered little in attack – a Flo header from a Zola free-kick that caused little danger being their sole contribution – but a brief rally saw Schmeichel called upon to deny Nicholls and Petrescu.

The Chelsea revival, however, was short-lived, as just on half-time, United struck again. A pass from Leboeuf was cut out by Pallister and the move continued with Giggs finding an unmarked Cole on the halfway line. Racing forward, he drew de Goey from his goal before chipping the ball over the diving 'keeper.

Gullit tried to reorganise his team after the break, pushing Le Saux forward from defence and Hughes up front, and they had their moments, although they still failed to get the better of Schmeichel. The big 'keeper denied Duberry and Zola, while Le Saux hit the post amid a goalmouth scramble.

But it all made little difference to the rampant United side as they increased their lead in the sixty-sixth minute. A Giggs pass sent Cole in between Leboeuf and Duberry to claim his seventeenth goal in sixteen games.

Eight minutes later, it was 5-0 and the signal for many of the home support to head for the exits. Beckham received a Giggs corner and was allowed too much space from some poor defending, before finding Sheringham, who headed home.

With sixteen minutes remaining, there was little chance of Chelsea causing something of an upset, or even forcing a replay but, rather surprisingly, United took their foot off the pedal and allowed their concentration to waver, giving Chelsea the opportunity of obtaining some hint of respectability.

Le Saux pulled a goal back in the sixty-eighth minute with an exquisite chip over Schmeichel, after Clarke had hassled Beckham into making an error. Substitute Vialli then scored two in the final seven minutes, responding to the chants of 'we want two' from the home supporters who still remained. The first created by a fine run from Di Matteo, the second when he intercepted Pallister's attempted back pass and tried to set up Petrescu, only to beat Schmeichel himself.

In between, Di Matteo missed an excellent opportunity, as did Beckham, then at the final whistle a mass confrontation between around a dozen players ended with Le Saux and Sheringham being booked.

It was later reported that ill feeling had been simmering since half-time when Beckham and Leboeuf came head to head in the tunnel following a running battle that had flared up seconds before the break, when the Chelsea player had fouled Cole and Beckham had become involved.

'United in a different class,' proclaimed the heading above the match report in the *Daily Express*, with Alex Ferguson admitting that he knew prior to the game that his team would destroy their opponents. 'I knew we had the battle won when I looked at the team sheets,' said the United manager. 'It's easy for people to say that our priorities are the European Cup or the Premiership, and they might be right. But when you go away to Chelsea in the FA Cup, there's always a sense of anticipation among my players.

'That energises them and their true character comes out. They want to win these kind of games and they wanted to win today because we were serious and focussed purely on this game.'

He continued, 'I played my maximum team today and we started superbly. We weren't going to be intimidated or second best to any ball and when you have that platform, attacking comes naturally.

'It's a long season and we will get better in terms of consistency. You have to do that if you want to win the Premiership.'

24

Nottingham Forest (A)

6 February 1999

It was the forty-first anniversary of the Munich disaster, everyone conjuring up the memories of that wonderful side, and with each passing year those thoughts did not come any easier to bear. There was also another topic of conversation among the travelling United support on their way to Nottingham, surrounding the appointment of Steve McLaren as Alex Ferguson's new assistant manager.

Steve who?

McLaren had joined United, replacing Brian Kidd who had left in December, from just a few miles along the road where he was about to take his place on the visitors' bench for the first time, having been assistant manager at Derby County since June 1995. As a player he had begun his career with Hull City, joining Derby in 1985, later moving to Bristol City and Oxford United, where he began coaching.

Strangely enough, Ferguson himself had come under scrutiny for the vacant England job, but would only say 'I refuse to discuss the situation' when asked.

For McLaren and Ferguson, their immediate priority was to consolidate United's place at the top of the Premiership, where they held a four-point advantage over Chelsea, although they had played a game more.

Nottingham Forest: Beasant, Harkes, Palmer, Hjelde, Armstrong, Stone, Gemmill, Johnson, Rogers (1), van Hooijdonk, Darcheville. Substitutes: Porfirio for Armstrong, Freedman for Darcheville and Mattsson for Gemmil. Crossley and Bart-Williams not used.
United: Schmeichel, G. Neville, Johnsen, Stam, P. Neville, Beckham, Keane, Scholes, Blomqvist, Cole (2), Yorke (2). Substitutes: Curtis for Keane, Butt for Blomqvist and Solskjaer (4) for Yorke. Van der Gouw and May not used.
Score: 8-1
Attendance: 30,025

United made four changes to the side that had defeated McLaren's old club 1-0 three days previously, bringing in Cole, Beckham, Phil Neville and Blomqvist in place of Solskjaer, Butt, Irwin and Giggs, but those changes were to make little difference to the performance and momentum of the team.

For anyone late in arriving at the City Ground, there was a good possibility that they might have missed the opening three goals, all scored in a whirlwind opening seven minutes. Straight from the kick-off, United swarmed forward and, in their first attack, Dwight Yorke notched his twentieth goal of the season in the second minute, Beckham's corner going high over the players cluttered in the penalty area, but being picked up by Keane on the by-line. Cutting the ball back to Scholes, the midfielder chipped it forward into the Forest penalty area where Yorke stole in and marked to side-foot it home.

Allowing their minds to wander following this early goal, Ron Atkinson's Forest quickly retaliated and drew level four minutes later, cutting through the United defence with ease. Rogers played a one-two with Darcheville and the former shot across Schmeichel and into the far corner.

Congratulating themselves at springing immediately back into the game, Forest were then hit with a sucker punch sixty seconds later, when United regained the advantage.

A long ball from Keane direct from the restart found the Forest defence all at sea and in stepped Andy Cole to claim his sixteenth of the season, although it is debatable as to whether or not it was the United player or Hjelde who got the last touch before the ball crossed the line.

Beckham was a constant danger, his crosses causing countless problems, and from one Cole thought he had scored his seventeenth of the season, but the referee waved play on, dismissing claims that the ball had crossed the line.

Forest, to their credit, once again fought back, seeking an immediate equaliser, and Schmeichel was forced into making an excellent save to maintain United's lead. Rogers cut out an attempted cross-field pass from Scholes and moved forward before crossing towards van Hooijdonk, but the Dutchman's shot was superbly stopped by the big Dane.

United, however, began to run the game, with their forwards in fine form.

Cole shot narrowly wide in the twenty-sixth minute, after chesting down a long through pass from Beckham, but for all their advantage, they could not increase their two-goal advantage before the interval.

Seconds after the restart, Scholes picked up the ball some 30 yards from goal and sent a thunderous drive against the Forest crossbar with Beasant well beaten, but it was to take only four minutes before that third goal materialised, when Beasant failed to hold a shot from Yorke, with Cole nipping quickly in to nudge the ball under the 'keeper and into the vacant net.

Freedman was denied by Schmeichel and then sent a 25-yard effort narrowly over as the home side continued to chase the game. But United went 4-1 in front in the sixty-seventh minute through the other member of their dynamic front duo, Yorke pouncing on the ball 3 yards out after Hjelde had diverted Blomqvist's cross onto his own post.

Five minutes later, the fun really started, when United substituted Solskjaer for Yorke, although it was eight minutes before the Norwegian was to increase United's lead, scoring from Gary Neville's right-wing cross.

Before you had time to catch your breath, he had put United 6-1 in front. Attempting to chip Beasant, the ball fell back to him and this time he made no mistake. With three minutes remaining, the game was well and truly out of Forest's reach, as the Norwegian claimed his hat-trick, a mishit shot from Scholes falling invitingly.

Full time beckoned. It looked all over, but there was no relaxing within the United ranks and Butt crossed towards the far post and Solskjaer scored his fourth and United's eighth, making four goals in the space of thirteen minutes.

'Big Ron for England,' chanted the away support. Few teams would have lived with United in this form, with all three strikers on top of their game.

'It's a good job Ryan Giggs didn't play, otherwise we might have got a real spanking,' said Ron Atkinson with a rueful smile.

It was the biggest away win in the Premiership to date, beating, strangely enough, Forest's 7-1 win over Sheffield Wednesday in 1995, while it was also a scoreline exceeded twice previously by an away side – in December 1908 when Sunderland won 9-1 at Newcastle and in season 1955/56 when Wolves beat Cardiff City by the same score. United now held the Premiership record for both the biggest wins at home and away, adding this result to their 9-0 victory over Ipswich Town at Old Trafford in March 1995.

Alex Ferguson was full of praise for his four-goal hero. 'Fantastic', 'marvellous', 'amazing', he exclaimed.

'There is no doubt about that. We have tried to playing him out on the left, but he is better as a central striker. That is where he prefers to play.'

Speaking about the game as a whole, he said, 'It is the best display of finishing in my time at United and, in terms of goal potential, we've never been stronger.'

25

Arsenal (N)

14 April 1999

When it came to drama, in the chase for the treble, the FA Cup certainly did not want left out of the equation. Having disposed of Middlesbrough 3-1, Liverpool 2-1 with a last gasp Solskjaer winner, Fulham 1-0 and Chelsea 2-0, after a 0-0 draw at Old Trafford, it was two semi-finals in the space of four days, with the Champions League semi-final first-leg tie against Juventus at Old Trafford preceding the trip to Villa Park to face Arsenal in the last four of the FA Cup.

Against the Italians, United were held to a 1-1 draw. Not the best of results, but it did leave everything to play for in the second leg. In the Midlands, Alex Ferguson's team were again held to a draw, 0-0 this time around, robbed of a place in the Wembley final at the first attempt by a linesman's flag.

Beckham pushed the ball down the wing to Giggs, and up went the flag, but not for the Welshman to have moved too far forward, but for Yorke, in an offside position in the centre. As Giggs moved down the flank, the flag went down, the ball was centred and Keane slammed the ball into the roof of the net.

At first the referee awarded a goal, but then noticed the flag was again raised and, after a brief conversation, a free-kick was awarded to Arsenal.

Even extra time could not separate the two teams, so it was back to Villa Park three days later, Newcastle United awaiting the victors at Wembley.

Arsenal: Seaman, Dixon, Keown, Adams, Winterburn, Parlour, Viera, Petit, Ljungberg, Bergkamp (1), Anelka. Substitutes: Kanu for Parlour, Bould for Petit and Overmars for Ljungberg. Lukic and Vivas not used.
United: Schmeichel, G. Neville, Stam, Johnsen, P. Neville, Beckham (1), Keane, Butt, Blomqvist, Solskjaer, Sheringham. Substitutes: Giggs (1) for Blomqvist, Yorke for Solskjaer and Scholes for Sheringham. Van der Gouw and Irwin not used.
Score: 2-1
Attendance: 30,223

With much to play for in the Champions League semi-final against Juventus the following week, Alex Ferguson decided to take something of a risk and leave both Andy Cole and Dwight Yorke out of his starting eleven. A gamble perhaps, but one that was to certainly pay off.

But at Villa Park in the FA Cup semi-final replay, there was also a great deal at stake and the opening period was somewhat flat and uneventful, the lull before the storm, as play was cautious, with neither side willing to attempt anything too adventurous. Something eventually had to give and in the seventeenth minute the game took on a new meaning.

Schmeichel cleared his lines, hoping to find Solskjaer, but instead it fell towards Keown, whose attempt to head clear landed at the feet of Beckham, 40 yards out. A quick one-two with Sheringham and the ball was soon flying past a helpless Seaman and into the left-hand corner of the net.

The game had woken from its rather lazy start and Arsenal were soon searching for an equaliser. Within four minutes, Bergkamp had forced a diving save out of Schmeichel, then Parlour cut inside past Johnsen and attempted to beat the United 'keeper from 16 yards out, but the big Dane was equal to the Arsenal man's effort.

Sheringham tried his luck with a low shot from a Blomqvist cross and minutes later with a header from a Beckham free-kick, neither of which were to cause Seaman any real problems.

Slowly, the pace of the game increased, as did the tempers, with Stam, Keane, Beckham and Keown all booked within a ten-minute spell, as Arsenal began to come more and more into the game. Schmeichel was again called into action, having to dash from his goal to thwart Petit and then Anelka, having beaten two United defenders, wasted the opportunity by driving the ball into the side netting.

So United held the advantage at the interval and did so until the sixty-ninth minute, but as the second half got underway, they should have punished the Gunners for some shoddy play. As the Gunners hadn't taken advantage of the situation, they were duly punished.

Bergkamp picked the ball up some 20 yards out and, moving infield, shot for goal. The ball clipped the leg of Stam and beat Schmeichel's desperate dive. The goal knocked the game up a few notches, as did an Anelka effort being disallowed for offside, as he pounced on Bergkamp shot that the United 'keeper failed to hold.

The howls of disapproval from the Arsenal following were soon to be replaced in the seventy-third minute, but a few decibels louder, by those of the United support, when Keane received his second yellow card for upending Overmars.

Time was slowly running out, but with extra time once again beckoning, Phil Neville rather clumsily challenged Parlour in the United area. Down went the Arsenal man and referee David Elleray immediately pointed to the penalty spot.

As Bergkamp placed the ball on the spot, few United supporters, or even players for that matter, would have expected him to miss, but his kick was rather poorly struck. Schmeichel dived the correct way and kept his team in the hunt.

Even though there was the additional half-hour to play, it would not have been too unexpected had Schmeichel been called upon to face further penalties by the end of the night, but he was to be spared the trouble.

It was the 109th minute of this compelling semi-final as Viera attempted a cross-field pass which, by his standards, was poorly timed. Just inside his own half, Giggs picked up the loose ball and moved over the halfway line, drifting rather effortlessly past Viera, trying to make amends for his error, and full-back Dixon.

With Yorke having run to the left of Giggs in an attempt to distract Keown, the Welshman held off the challenge of the backtracking Dixon and, as Adams moved in with an attempt to block the ball, Giggs rifled the ball above the head of Seaman and into the roof of the net.

It was a goal of the highest standards, one of the greatest goals of the modern game. Giggs pulled off his white shirt and retraced his 60-yard run, but on this occasion evading pitch-encroaching jubilant United supporters instead of red-shirted Arsenal defenders.

United were Wembley bound.

'Genius,' said a delighted United manager. 'It's his balance that gives him a real chance of being truly great,' and it was that un-coachable quality that enabled him to glide through the best defence in Europe.

'He can wrong-foot anybody just by movement. Just when you think a tackler is going to get to the ball, he seems to float or ride over the challenge.

'In terms of coming in an important game, that goal stands alone.'

Of the game itself, Alex Ferguson was quick to point out that 'the semi-final was about getting through no matter what because of the importance of the game'.

26

Juventus (A)

21 April 1999

'This game against Juventus is the biggest – and I have a genuine feeling that we can win it,' said a hyped-up Alex Ferguson prior to the Champions League semi-final second leg.

'When we lost to Borussia Dortmund we should have got to the final. But I was never quite sure whether the team were ready to win the European Cup then.

'We would still have had to handle that atmosphere and the experience of playing Juventus in the final.

'Now you can just feel that we are capable of playing against anyone. We have more control and patience about our game.

'There are people in life who are quite happy to settle for what they have. Other people, though, are achievers. They are always chasing the next part of their success story. They want to progress all the time.

'In fairness to Manchester United, it has a tradition of having players with courage, fighters.'

Juventus: Peruzzi, Birindelli, Ferrara, Iuliano, Pessotto, Conte, Descamps, Davids, Di Livio, Zidane, Inzaghi (2). Substitutes: Fonseca for Di Livio, Montero for Iuliano and Amoruso for Birindelli. Rampulla, Tudor, Tacchinardi and Esnaider not used.
United: Schmiechel, G. Neville, Irwin, Johnsen, Stam, Beckham, Butt, Blomqvist, Keane (1), Yorke (1), Cole (1). Substitutes: Scholes for Blomqvist. Van der Gouw, May, Sheringham, P. Neville, Solskjaer and Brown not used.
Score: 3-2
Attendance: 65,500

United were certainly going to need courage, along with skill, determination and an element of luck, if they were going to overcome the Italian giants and progress into the Champions League final for only the second time in the club's history.

The 1-1 draw at Old Trafford perhaps favoured Juventus more than United, as they had the advantage of that all-too-important away goal, but it was certainly not something that overly concerned the visitors. An injury to Ryan Giggs, which forced him out of Alex Ferguson's team selection, was considerably more worrying, as a repeat of his wonder goal against Arsenal would have been only too welcome.

The game, however, got off to the worst possible start for United, amid the constant drumbeats and red flares, as Juventus went ahead in only the sixth minute. Zidane had threatened early on, flicking the ball over the head of Stam, but the United central defender regained his composure and managed to block the Frenchman's route to goal. But soon afterwards, it was from a Zidane cross that Juventus took the lead.

Beckham, back in a defensive role, conceded a corner, and as Zidane played it short to Di Livio, he took the return and his cross flashed into the United area, where Inzaghi sneaked in front of Gary Neville to beat Schmeichel from close in.

An overhead kick from Cole was stopped on the line by goalkeeper Peruzzi, but this was something of an isolated moment at that end of the pitch, as Juventus were controlling those early stages.

With eleven minutes gone, they were 2-0 in front. Davids found Inzaghi, who was giving the United defence a torrid time, with an inch-perfect pass. Although he had his back to goal and covered by Stam, he somehow managed to turn; his shot took a deflection off Stam and spun over the head of Schmeichel and into the net.

3-1 down and even at this early stage, the game seemed way beyond United's reach.

Yorke and Cole combined in the nineteenth minute, but the former's shot was well off target, then Yorke was brought down by Iuliano as he ran through. As the ball broke to Beckham, the referee waved play on, but the midfielder could not get the better of the Italian 'keeper.

But five minutes later the visitors were back in the game.

Cole's cross was deflected for a corner, and from Beckham's kick on the right, the ball was met by Keane and his glancing header at the near post flew into the net.

On the half-hour, Juventus almost increased their lead when Schmeichel missed a Zidane cross as he was challenged in mid-air by Conte, but the Italian's header was cleared off the line by Stam.

Keane's header had given United renewed hope, but the United captain's hopes of lifting the Champions League trophy were banished in the thirty-second minute when he was booked by the Swiss referee for a foul on Zidane. Fortunate to have escaped a booking for a foul on Davids earlier, this booking was enough to rule the Irishman out of the final.

Against all odds, United drew level in the thirty-fourth minute. Having collected a Beckham pass, Cole sent a perfect cross towards the head of his striking partner, Dwight Yorke, who dived forward to head home. United were now ahead in the tie for the first time.

The action swung from end to end, as Cole had a shot saved, as did Inzaghi, while Yorke hit the post with an angled drive.

The second half began with Inzaghi once again threatening the United defence, dashing into the penalty area only to be denied a hat-trick by the outstretched leg of Schmeichel. Then an Irwin error, just outside the United area, saw Inzaghi put a mishit effort past Schmeichel, only to see it disallowed for offside. United were certainly riding their luck.

The seventy-first minute found Irwin at the opposite end, where his firmly struck drive rebounded off the post and United's bad luck continued minutes later when

Scholes was booked for a trip on Deschamps. It was a yellow card that would also see the United midfielder miss the final, should United get there.

United continued to hang onto the slim advantage that they had, but then, with six minutes remaining, Yorke rounded Juventus 'keeper Peruzzi, only to be brought down. The ball rolled towards Cole, who seized the opportunity and slipped the loose ball into the Italian goal as the referee allowed the advantage to be played.

United were home and dry.

'To come to Juventus and to give the best club side in Europe over the last decade a two goal start and win the match was quite phenomenal,' exclaimed a delighted United manager.

'The first forty-five minutes is the best performance from a United side in my time in charge.

'I think we deserved it. We made it hard for ourselves but even at 2-0 down I thought we would do it.'

He was, however, to admit fearing the worst when Inzaghi scored his second, saying, 'I thought it was another case of suicide which has happened over the years.

'The difference is that this team has great composure. They composed themselves when they lost the second goal and started to express themselves very well.

'The disappointment for me is that Roy Keane and Paul Scholes will miss the final.

'It's a tragedy for them. I don't think it was a dirty match and I'm disappointed to lose two players of their standing. They were very unlucky.'

27

Tottenham Hotspur (H)

16 May 1999

Who knows how a season will unfold? You set out to win as many games as possible, but at the end of the day only one team can win the League and one team can win the cup.

But the 1998/99 season was like no other in the history of Manchester United Football Club. Come Sunday 16 May, United stood one point in front of Arsenal at the top of the FA Carling Premiership. Victory over the Gunners' north London rivals Tottenham Hotspur at Old Trafford would secure the title. Arsenal were at home to fifth-placed Aston Villa.

But that wasn't the complete picture.

The following Saturday, United were at Wembley, where they were due to meet Newcastle United in the FA Cup final, giving them the chance of securing the 'double'.

But perhaps more importantly, in ten days' time they had yet another ninety minutes to play out, against Bayern Munich in Barcelona, in the Champions League final.

Victory in all three fixtures would give them an unprecedented 'treble'. But as the old cliché said, let's take one game at a time.

'When I arrived in England thirteen years ago, Liverpool were the great rivals of United, but their last title was in 1989/90,' said Alex Ferguson. 'So Arsenal and ourselves have dominated the '90s, and it's come down to that situation again this season.'

He continued, 'What has been integral to my success at United was winning the League for the first time in 1993.

'It gave me longevity and it gave me control. Thereafter, you can pick the challenges you want without the pressure of trying to win a league for the first time, because that was the be-all end-all in my mind.

'After we won that first title, it seemed a great cloud was lifted from everyone. There was not such pressure on the players to produce. They can enjoy playing for Manchester United.'

Winning another title was the United manager's priority and he went on to say, 'A great measure of character is to see how people respond to adversity.

'My lads were hurt last season when Arsenal beat us to the title. We had a lead, but they put together an incredible run and if you do that at the end of a season, you deserve to win it.

'What will be a factor now is ability. And it's a better motivation for us knowing we need to win to be guaranteed the title.'

United: Schmeichel, G. Neville, May, Johnsen, Irwin, Beckham (1), Keane, Scholes, Giggs, Sheringham, Yorke. Substitutes: Butt for Scholes, P. Neville for Giggs and Cole (1) for Sheringham. Van der Gouw and Solskjaer not used.
Tottenham Hotspur: Walker, Carr, Scales, Campbell, Edinburgh, Anderton, Sherwood, Freund, Ginola, Ferdinand (1), Iversen. Substitutes: Young for Scales, Dominguez for Ginola and Sinton for Dominguez. Baardsen and Clemence not used.
Score: 2-1
Attendance: 55,189

United were inspired by the return of Roy Keane to the starting line-up following injury and their championship challenge received a boost after only nine minutes, when Tottenham's arguably most dangerous player, David Ginola, limped off. Arsenal's title hopes took something of a dent.

Yorke could have opened the scoring as early as the fourth minute, but Walker saved at the near post. Five minutes later, an attempted clearance from Walker cannoned off Yorke's shin and it was a relieved Tottenham 'keeper who watched as the ball rebounded across goal and bounced off the foot of a post back into his arms. But despite the steadying influence of Keane, United were to go behind in the twenty-fourth minute.

Tottenham 'keeper Walker launched a huge kick downfield. Iversen, who had already volleyed narrowly over, flicked a header past David May and Ferdinand shrugged off a challenge from Johnsen. As Schmeichel advanced from his goal, the Tottenham forward lifted the ball over the United goalkeeper and into the yawning net.

This was not in the script.

Frustration was already running high both on and off the pitch. Sheringham, playing against his former club, was booked for a foul on Campbell and was perhaps more than a little fortunate to remain on the pitch after following through on Dominguez. Nerves also seemed to be a major feature of United's performance, as so much hinged on this one game.

Walker was forced to make two stunning saves from Scholes, while Beckham wasted a good opportunity, heading a Giggs cross over the bar. Beckham, however, was to make amends for his shoddy finish three minutes before the interval.

Scholes dispossessed Sherwood and exchanged passes with Giggs as play moved forward. Yorke pulled Edinburgh wide and Scholes picked out Beckham with a sublime pass as the winger arrived on the edge of the Tottenham area. The finish was powerful, giving Walker little chance of stopping it, although he did manage to get a hand to the ball.

Relief filled the stadium, but there were still forty-five nerve-wracking minutes remaining.

The mood of optimism continued after the break, as it took United only three minutes to take the lead. Gary Neville's well measured forward pass was controlled by Cole, a second-half substitute for the tightrope-walking Sheringham, and swiftly despatched over the outstretched arm of Walker.

The Tottenham 'keeper saved another two efforts from Scholes, who then put another scoring opportunity wide, as did Butt. Yorke and Cole were also found wanting in front of goal when just one more would have calmed the nerves and put the destination of the title beyond any doubts.

Rare Tottenham attacks caused panic among the United support, as radios were checked for Arsenal's progress, their 1-0 lead being constantly relayed throughout the ground.

The remainder of the game seemed to move along at a snail's pace, but with Keane in sublime form, tidying up at the back, prompting his forwards from midfield, United were well in control, more concerned about conceding a goal than scoring one, happy to hang on to that solitary one-goal lead.

At the end, it was to prove enough. Players and supporters celebrated as one.

'It was a hanging-on job,' admitted the United manager.

'Titles are won over a year. We deserved our success. We are the best team in the country. They never give in.

'My players were hanging onto a whole season of hard work. It really hurt my players when they didn't win anything last season. But they got their act together and proved themselves.

'Winning the title does take pressure off us in a sense for the two games we have now got left. We know that we are going into next season's European Cup as champions. If the players think that the FA Cup is the lesser of the two targets ahead of us, if a lot of them start thinking about Barcelona, they will soon wake up when I pick my team for Wembley next Friday.

'This club is not about egos. It is about maintaining success, about building on the bedrock that was laid down by Sir Matt. That is why I will make sure that no one will get carried away.'

28

Bayern Munich (N)

26 May 1999

The following weekend it was off to Wembley for the FA Cup final against Newcastle United. I don't think there was anyone present who actually thought the Geordies would win, and United's 2-0 win was so easy that it was something of an embarrassment, although an excellent workout for the more important fixture the following Wednesday.

Victory over Newcastle had, of course, given United the League and FA Cup double, an excellent triumph in any season, but for 1998/99, it was only two-thirds of the club's total ambition. Everything now hinged on the events due to be played out in Barcelona, amid the impressive backdrop of the Nou Camp stadium.

'We have a great, great chance,' said Ferguson.

'I feel the country is behind us. I think we are as good as any English team that's been in the European Cup final.

'So we must have a great chance to surpass everyone else. The Italians have dominated Europe for the last few years but we can put our name on the list too.

'If we win, I will be the happiest man in the world.

'We know we have got many aces in our goalscorers, even though we will miss Roy Keane.

'But I know my team because I picked it on Sunday. I know we can do this.

'This game won't daunt my boys. They are special. I trust them. I believe in them.'

But when asked, 'What if United fail?' Ferguson replied, 'My lack of vanity precludes me from being gutted about it. What I've achieved as a manager stands for itself. Maybe I've had good luck. I don't know. But I am blessed with what I've won.

'It would be a terrible disappointment, of course it would and yes, I would be upset because we have a great chance of winning.'

Bayern Munich: Kahn, Matthaus, Linke, Kuffour, Babbel, Effenberg, Jeremies, Tarnat, Basler (1), Janker, Zickler. Substitutes: Fink for Matthaus, Salihamidzic for Bassler and Scholl for Zickler. Dreher, Helmer, Strunz and Dael not used.
United: Schmeichel, G. Neville, Stam, Johnsen, Irwin, Giggs, Butt, Beckham, Blomqvist, Yorke, Cole. Substitutes: Sheringham (1) for Blomqvist and Solskjaer (1) for Cole. Van der Gouw, P. Neville, May, Brown and Greening not used.
Score: 2-1
Attendance: 90,000

Of all fifty games included in this book, this was obviously the first pencilled in, but it is also the one that proves most difficult to write about, as everyone knows the story off by heart, whether they were there, watched it on television, or weren't even born.

My daughter said, 'Just write five words: "AND SOLSKJAER HAS WON IT!"' But even although it sums up that memorable evening, it simply does not do it justice.

Like most, I can remember the whole day as if it was yesterday and I doubt if there will ever be another like it. Certainly not in my time.

In the writing of this book, I have delved into my own personal archives of United newspaper cuttings and match reports and I will do so once again here, but I will let the newspaper headlines of the following day, which cost me a few pounds at Manchester airport and back home in Dumfries, sum up most of the story.

'They Thought It Was All Over', proclaimed the *Sun*, with a photograph of Ole Gunnar Solskjaer surrounded by jubilant teammates after scoring 'that goal' on the front page. Another issue of the same paper had 'Best of All Time' on the front, with the Scottish issue (half the price of the others I must add) saluting the United manager with 'Oh what a Knight – now it's got to be Sir Fergie as United triumph' with a two-page photograph of the United manager and his players with the trophy. The *Scottish Daily Express* was along similar lines with 'Arise, Sir Alex – miracle in Barcelona as Fergie's heroes triumph'. 'Champions' was enough of a back-page heading for the same paper. The English version simply said 'United' on the front and 'King of Europe' on the back.

'Miracle Man – Fergie leads United to an amazing European victory' and 'Ole Grail' were the front and back of the *Daily Record*. 'Pride of Britain' said the *Mirror* on its front page, while on the back, it was 'Immortals – Subs rout Germans to clinch the greatest comeback of all time'. The *Daily Star* was perhaps not quite so diplomatic with 'Hunbelievevable – Utd snatch Glory in dying seconds' on their front cover, with 'Greatest Night of My Life' on the back. This was referring to a quote from Alex Ferguson, not every United supporter.

'Drama at the death as United make football history' grabbed some front-page space on the *Guardian*, but strangely, the *Times* published a photograph of the Bayern Munich goal rather than one of the celebrating United players above their front page heading – 'The dream comes true for United'.

'United win treble with miracle double' was the *Independent*'s lead, with 'United's will to win seals place in history' on the back.

The *Daily Telegraph* readers were greeted with 'Ferguson admits "I had given up hope" before victory is snatched in injury time – Man Utd clinch the Treble in last seconds'. 'Solskjaer makes treble come true' preceded Henry Winter's match report.

The *Manchester Evening News* simply published a triumphant United team across its front and back pages, with 'Champions of Europe'.

I think you get the gist of the story from all that.

But it was not all straightforward, as Bayern Munich had taken the lead in the sixth minute through Basler, curling a free-kick through a gap in the United defensive wall and past Schmeichel, after Johnsen had bundled Janker off the ball just outside the United penalty area.

The Germans continued to dominate the game, Scholl hitting the post in the seventy-ninth minute and Janker the crossbar six minutes from time.

Without Keane and Scholes, United were indifferent and somewhat unimpressive. Blomqvist had failed to produce anything worthwhile on the wing and was replaced by Sheringham in the sixty-sixth minute, with Giggs moving out wide on the left and Beckham on the opposite flank. United began to have more of a purpose about their game, but still the Germans threatened.

As something of a last throw of the dice, Alex Ferguson threw on Solskjaer for Cole with ten minutes remaining. The Norwegian was capable of anything. Many, however, would have removed a defender and added the extra forward, but we had faith in Fergie.

But still United could not penetrate the German defence and slowly the minutes ticked away.

I remember looking up at the scoreboard, which showed eighty-nine minutes, and thinking 'well at least I have seen United in the Champions League final', then the fourth official signalled three minutes of added time. 'Come on lads, one last effort.'

Pushing forward, they won a corner over to my right. With nothing to lose, the green jersey of Peter Schmeichel came lumbering up the field and into the German penalty area. Uncertain as to his presence, there was suddenly a sign of hesitancy in the German defence and a flicker of hope among the United support scattered around the ground. Beckham, as usual, swung the ball over and it was sliced clear as panic ensued. Yorke nodded the ball back towards Giggs, who half hit it back towards Khan's goal, where Sheringham swept it home.

The German heads went down immediately, as extra time loomed, but unlike most teams, United threw caution to the wind and, as the Bayern Munich players failed to retain possession following the restart, United surged forward again.

Gary Neville forced another corner on the left and once again Beckham swung the ball over. This time there was no Schmeichel, but the ball did find the head of Sheringham, who nodded it down towards the back post. Before anyone could react, Solskjaer stuck out a foot and the ball rose into the roof of the net. United had done it. There was no time for a comeback by the Germans. The Bayern Munich players weren't even up to restarting the game.

Such was the closeness of the goals that many were still celebrating the first when the second went in. I was working in a neighbouring town at the time and got a lift to work with two women with no interest in football. One, however, watched the game simply because I was there. As the ninetieth minute approached, she decided that enough was enough and went upstairs to get ready for bed. When Sheringham scored, her husband shouted up to her 'United have scored', a minute later he shouted up again 'United have scored', to which she replied, 'I heard you the first bloody time.' Priceless!

It was also a priceless moment for Alex Ferguson.

'I can't believe it,' he exclaimed. 'Football, bloody football. This is amazing. My boys just never gave in that's why we won it. Unbelievable. I'm so proud of my players.'

'It's fantastic. My players are incredible human beings. You can talk about tactics, but when you have got that spirit it's incredible.

'I knew we were going to miss Roy Keane and I did not think we played as well as we have been recently. But I still think we were the better team.

'We lost our way a bit in the last thirty minutes when we were chasing an equaliser and they hit us on the counter-attack.

'But then Teddy Sheringham and Ole Gunnar came on and it was magic. The players will not rest on what they have done.'

Arsenal (H)

25 February 2001

The top of the Premiership table had a not-unfamiliar look about it on the morning of 25 February 2001, with United on top with sixty-three points from twenty-seven games and Arsenal hanging onto their coat tails, but some thirteen points adrift. Liverpool were a distant third, eighteen points behind. Sir Alex Ferguson's team were edging closer to their seventh Premiership crown.

Arsenal manager Arsène Wenger admitted he was 'embarrassed and responsible – probably like a few other managers – that we are so far behind. It hurts to have let them get so far ahead. The other teams have been inconsistent while United have the ability to win matches even when they have not played very well.'

With three months of the season remaining and some ten games still to play, the title chase could still offer some twists and turns, but a victory, or indeed a draw, against second-placed Arsenal at Old Trafford would all but write off any hopes the Londoners had of derailing United's celebrations.

United: Barthez, G. Neville, Silvestre, Stam, Brown, Beckham, Keane (1), Butt, Scholes, Yorke (3), Solskjaer (1). Substitutes: Chadwick for Keane and Sheringham (1) for Yorke. Rachubka, Irwin and P. Neville not used.
Arsenal: Seaman, Luzhny, Stepanovs, Grimandi Cole, Pires, Parlour, Viera, Silvinho, Wiltord, Henry (1). Substitutes: Ljungberg for Cole and Vivas for Parlour. Manninger, Bergkamp and Kanu not used.
Score: 6-1
Attendance: 67,535

If Arsène Wenger had any hopes of catching United as the Arsenal team bus approached Old Trafford prior to kick-off, then they were soon to evaporate as the game got underway, and he was about to discover why his team were playing second fiddle to United.

Arsenal, in the past renowned for their defensive capabilities, were without the likes of Adams, Keown and Dixon, with the nondescript Stepanovs, Grimandi and an out-of-sorts Ashley Cole left to face the wrath of Dwight Yorke and Ole Gunnar Solskjaer, but even with the more established rearguard, the Gunners would have struggled.

With a mere two minutes on the clock and the crowd still settling down, the theme for the afternoon was set. Beckham crossed from the right, Scholes dummied and the ball fell to Yorke. The United striker pushed the ball back out to Scholes near the touchline. Returning the compliment as the Arsenal defence stood stationary, Yorke slipped the ball past Seaman with his knee for his first goal since New Year's Day.

Although shaken by this early setback, Arsenal, to their credit, responded as title challengers should, pulling a goal back in the sixteenth minute.

Wiltord and Pires worked the ball down the United right and, with the home defence looking as stable as the visitors, Henry tucked away the eventual cross to level the score.

Many felt that United would now have a fight on their hands if they wanted to increase their top-of-the-table advantage, but it was not to be, as within two minutes they had reclaimed their advantage.

Making only his second start in nine games, Dwight Yorke moved onto a Roy Keane pass, floated over the top of the Arsenal defence and beat Seaman with a shot on the run.

A further two minutes and Yorke claimed his hat-trick, having already been denied a third by Seaman, who pushed a header over the bar, drumming out a clear message to the suspended Andy Cole. Set up by Beckham, Yorke picked up the ball in his own area, outstripped Stepanovs before beating Seaman with ease.

The goals were coming thick and fast, as only a further three minutes had elapsed before United were 4-1 in front. Yorke once again tormented Stepanovs before setting up Roy Keane, who chested the ball down before driving home from 15 yards out.

The Arsenal defending was, at times, a farce, and in the thirty-seventh minute, Grimandi added to the Keystone Cops approach by falling over, allowing Nicky Butt to pick out Solskjaer who, unchallenged, slotted home United's fifth.

Four goals behind, there was no way that Arsenal could claw themselves back into the game. Wenger pulled Silvinho back from midfield into a more defensive role, but it was somewhat unnecessary, as United took their foot off the pedal in the second forty-five minutes.

United could have added more, rubbing in their superiority, but with such a commanding lead, it is difficult to maintain such a pressure as the game moves towards its conclusion.

Seaman had been taunted 'England's number one' with every goal, while the arrival of Teddy Sheringham limbering up down the touchline fifteen minutes from time at least gave the Arsenal support, or those who were still in the ground, something to shout about, releasing a torrent of abuse at the former Tottenham striker. The United substitute took it all in his stride, waving five fingers in the direction of the away support with a huge smile on his face.

The smile became bigger and the five fingers became six in the final minute when, after hitting the post a minute earlier, he added the sixth from 20 yards out.

'One-Six to the Arsenal,' chanted the crowd, but there were, by now, few left in the away area.

'We defended as a youth team,' muttered an 'ashamed' Arsène Wenger, while his opposite number said, 'I think Arsenal are finished in the League, but it would still be silly to talk about winning it.

'We still have games against Leeds and Liverpool to come and I don't want my players to relax.

'They are always better when they are playing on the edge and we still have some work to do.'

He continued, 'I want to win the title in the proper manner and to achieve that, the players will need to stay focused.

'It was a very surprising scoreline because recent games between ourselves and Arsenal have been very close. I never expected a result like that.'

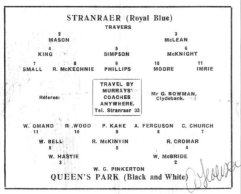

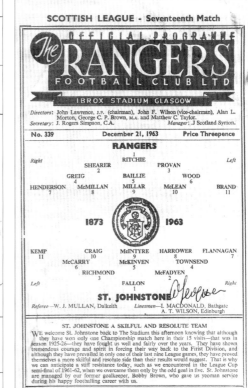

Above left: 1. Programme from Stranraer *v.* Queens Park, 15 November 1958.

Above right: 2. Programme from Rangers *v.* St Johnstone, 21 December 1963.

Below: 3. Ticket from Aberdeen *v.* Real Madrid, 11 May 1983.

Right: 4. Programme from the game *v.* Oxford United, 8 November 1986.

Above left: 5. Programme from the game *v.* Somerset Trojans, 1 December 1987.

Above right: 6. Programme for the game *v.* Liverpool, 4 April 1988.

Left: 7. Matchday programme for the game *v.* Wimbledon, 2 May 1989.

Below: 8. Ticket for the game *v.* Manchester City, 23 September 1989.

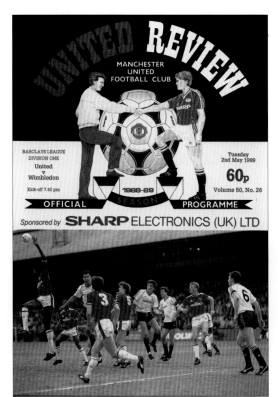

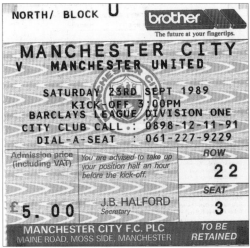

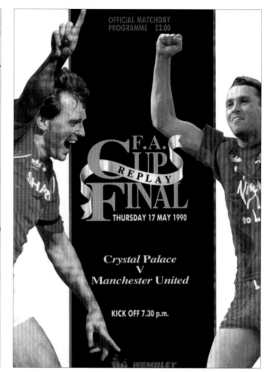

Above left: 9. Ticket from the game *v.*
Nottingham Forest, 7 January 1990.

Above right: 10. Programme for the replay *v.*
Crystal Palace, 17 May 1990.

Below: 11. Ticket for the game *v.* Queens Park
Rangers, 1 January 1992.

Right: 12. Programme for the game *v.* FC
Barcelona, 15 May 1991.

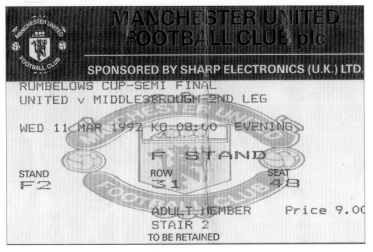

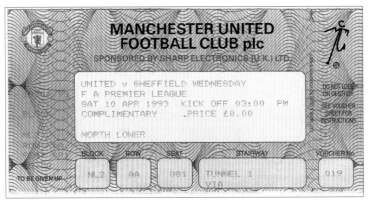

Top left: 13. Ticket for the game against Middlesbrough, 11 March 1992.

Left: 14. Ticket for the game *v.* Sheffield Wednesday, 10 April 1993.

Below left: 15. Ticket for the semi-final tie *v.* Oldham Athletic, 10 April 1994.

Below right: 16. Ticket for the game *v.* Port Vale, 27 September 1994.

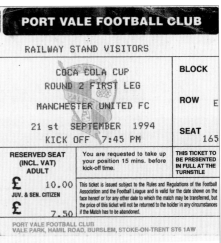

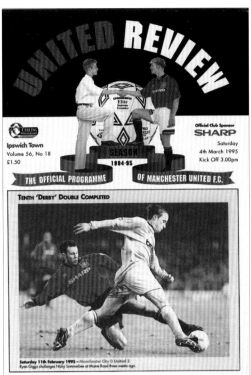

Above left: 17. Ticket for the match *v.* Crystal Palace, 25 January 1995.

Above right: 18. Matchday programme for the game *v.* Ipswich Town, 4 March 1995.

Right: 19. Ticket for the match *v.* West Ham United, 14 May 1995.

Below right: 20. Ticket for the match *v.* Aston Villa, 19 August 1995.

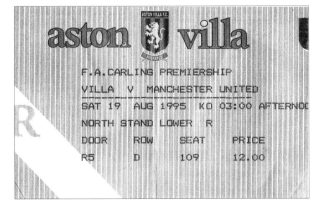

21. Ticket for the game
v. Southampton on
13 April 1996.

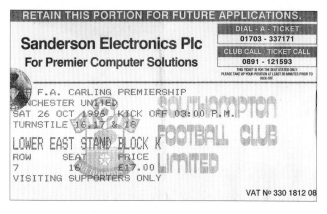

22. Ticket for the game
v. Southampton on
26 October 1996.

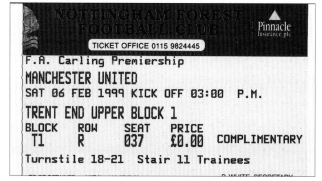

23. Ticket for the match
v. Nottingham Forest,
6 February 1999.

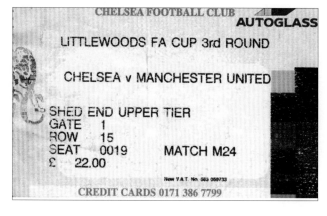

24. Ticket for the game *v.*
Chelsea, 4 January 1998.

Above left: 25. Ticket from the match *v.* Juventus, 21 April 1999.

Top right: 26. Ticket from the match *v.* Arsenal, 14 April 1999.

Above right: 27. Ticket from the match *v.* Tottenham Hotspur, 29 September 1999.

Below: 28. The Champions League final *v.* Bayern Munich, 26 May 1999. (Kenny Ramsey)

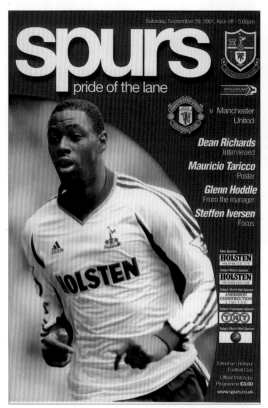

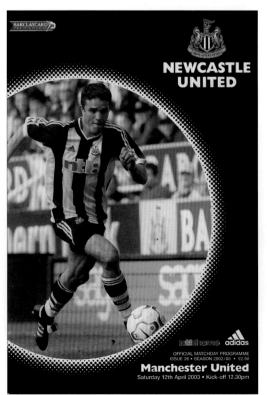

Above left: 29. Matchday programme for the game *v.* Tottenham Hotspur, 29 September 2001.

Above right: 30. Ticket for the game *v.* Arsenal, 25 February 2001.

Left: 31. Matchday programme for the game *v.* Newcastle United, 12 April 2003.

32. Ticket for the game *v.* Real Madrid, 23 April 2003.

33. Ticket for the game *v.* Bolton Wanderers, 16 August 2003.

34. Ticket for the game *v.* Fenerbahce, 28 September 2004.

35. Ticket for the game *v.* Wigan Athletic, 26 February 2006.

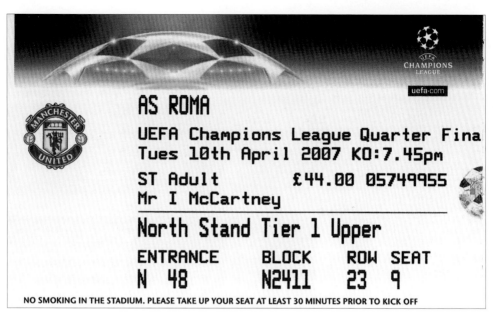

AS ROMA

UEFA Champions League Quarter Fina
Tues 10th April 2007 KO:7.45pm

ST Adult   £44.00 05749955
Mr I McCartney

North Stand Tier 1 Upper

ENTRANCE   BLOCK   ROW SEAT
N 48   N2411   23   9

NO SMOKING IN THE STADIUM. PLEASE TAKE UP YOUR SEAT AT LEAST 30 MINUTES PRIOR TO KICK OFF

Above: 36. Ticket for the game *v.* Roma, 10 April 2007.

Below left: 37. Programme for the match *v.* Chelsea, 21 May 2008.

Below right: 38. Ticket for the match *v.* Liga de Quito, 21 December 2008.

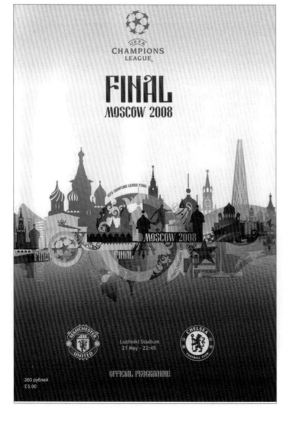

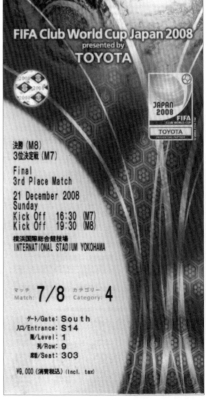

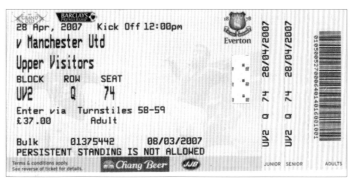

39. Ticket for the game *v.* Everton, 28 April 2007.

40. Ticket for the game *v.* Aston Villa, 5 April 2009.

41. Ticket for the game *v.* Manchester City, 20 April 2009.

42. Ticket for the game *v.* Blackpool, 25 January 2011, postponed from 4 December 2010.

43. Matchday programme for the game *v.* Chelsea, 8 May 2011.

44. Matchday programme for the game *v.* Manchester City, 23 October 2011.

CHAMPIONS

ENGLISH LEAGUE CHAMPIONS FOR A RECORD 19TH TIME

Arsenal

Barclays Premier League

Sun 28 Aug 2011   Kick Off 4pm

East Stand Tier 2

Entrance	Block	Row	Seat	Price
E 32	E332	8	140	£37.00

Mrs L McCartney   478529 / 84758398

Adult (Member)

  MANUTD.COM
0161 868 8000

 Manchester
City
Football
Club

ETIHAD
AIRWAYS
TAILORED by UMBRO

ADULT

Barclays Premier League
Sun 09 December 2012 13:30

Manchester City FC vs Manchester United FC

Visiting Supporter   05910675

Aisle: 114   Block: 114   Row: T   Seat: 359

Entrance: M   Price: 51.00

05910675
Valid for adult unless stub removed

Top: 45. Ticket for the game *v.* Arsenal, 28 August 2011.

Middle: 46. Ticket for the game *v.* Manchester City, 9 December 2012.

Right: 47. Programme for the game *v.* Newcastle United, 26 December 2012.

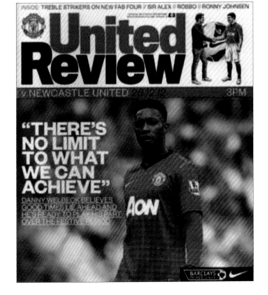

Above: 48. Ticket for the game *v.* Swansea City, 12 May 2013.

Below left: 49. Matchday programme for the game *v.* Aston Villa, 22 April 2013.

Below right: 50. Matchday programme for Sir Alex Ferguson's final game, *v.* West Bromwich Albion, 19 May 2013.

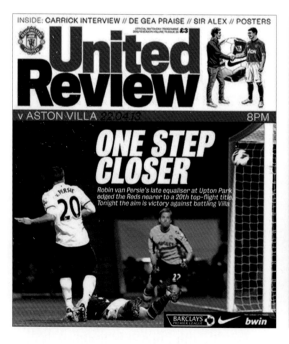

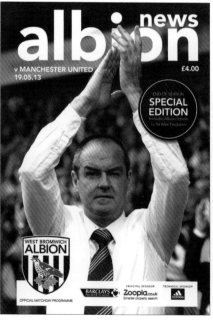

51. The statue of Sir Alex Ferguson outside Old Trafford.

SIR ALEX FERGUSON

Above and below: 52 & 53. The Sir Alex Ferguson Stand.

30

Tottenham Hotspur (A)

29 September 2001

Having announced that he was going retire at the end of the 2001/02 season, Sir Alex Ferguson was wanting to leave Old Trafford in a blaze of glory, having added more silverware to United's neverending list of honours, but with the new season only a matter of weeks old, it was beginning to look as though he had a considerable amount of work to do.

A trip to Spain to play Deportivo in a Champions League Group G fixture saw his team beaten 2-1, while after-match rumours suggested a major dressing room bust-up between Roy Keane and recent signing Ruud van Nistelrooy.

The United manager was also in something of a quandary as to how best utilise his £28-million signing Sebastian Veron.

Thankfully, a 3-1 victory over Ipswich Town the previous Saturday had kept United in a challenging position in the Premiership, sitting in third place, a point behind early leaders Bolton Wanderers.

Next up was a trip to London and White Hart Lane, a ground where United had enjoyed a mixture of results amid some compelling fixtures. The latest ninety minutes between the two clubs was to conjure up as memorable a game as any of the previous meetings.

Tottenham Hotspur: Sullivan, Perry, Richards (1), King, Tarricco, Poyet, Freund, Anderton, Ziege (1), Sherringham, Ferdinand (1). Substitutes: Rebrov for Anderton. Keller, Thelwell, Davies and Etherington not used.
United: Barthez, G. Neville, Blanc (1), Johnsen, Irwin, Beckham (1), Butt, Veron (1), Scholes, van Nistelrooy (1), Cole (1). Substitutes: Solskjaer for Butt and Silvestre for Irwin. Carroll, P. Neville and Chadwick not used.
Score: 5-3
Attendance: 36,038

If ever there was a game of football for the neutral, or one to advertise everything good about the game, then this was it. Indeed, it was also the perfect example of the 'game of two halves'.

United of course, were the reigning champions, and it was no secret that everyone would put in that little bit of extra effort to get the better of the team wearing the crown. Tottenham were no different and turned on a pulsating forty-five minutes of football, which left their visitors reeling and 3-0 down at half-time.

Fifteen minutes gone and Tottenham took the lead. Debutant Dean Richards drifted away from Gary Neville and headed Darren Anderton's corner firmly past a helpless Fabien Barthez.

The exposed United defence was found wanting once again ten minutes later when Poyet picked out Les Ferdinand, who left Blanc stranded as the Frenchman tried to spring the offside trap, before hitting a low shot past Barthez.

Further sloppy defending, this time by David Beckham, allowed Christian Ziege to add a third in stoppage time, diving to head home yet another pinpoint Poyet cross-field pass from 6 yards out.

Interval conversation all pointed to a Tottenham victory and, indeed, how many they could actually score.

A radio station was also in the process of putting together a programme entitled 'United in Crisis'.

But Tottenham were not counting their chickens, or their good fortune in finding the United defence on yet another off day, as only a fortnight previously Ferguson's team had gone to Newcastle and gone 3-1 down before scoring twice in a minute to get right back into the game, only to concede a fourth. Could they do so again?

A rib injury to Nicky Butt in the fortieth minute had already forced the United manager's hand and, with nothing to lose, when already 2-0 down, he threw on an extra forward in Solskjaer. Perhaps not exactly a master stroke, but it was certainly to provide dividends. Replacing Irwin with Silvestre was also to pay dividends.

A few long-range efforts had been the sum total of United's first-half attempts, but within a minute of the restart, they had pulled a goal back, Neville collected a Beckham pass and from his cross, Andy Cole sent a diving header past Sullivan at the near post.

Suddenly, it was like a switch had been flicked and United sprang into life, while Tottenham for some reason began to show some hesitancy in their play.

Solskjaer headed narrowly wide, Beckham fired over and, despite Tottenham's defence being well equipped to deal with high balls, United persisted with firing high crosses into the Spurs area. It was from a Beckham corner that Blanc headed home a second in the fifty-eighth minute, following continued pressure on the home goal.

It was then Johnsen's turn to head wide from a Beckham corner, and then Beckham himself put a left-footed shot narrowly wide, as Veron began to control midfield. Yet another header put United level nineteen minutes from time, Silvestre making ground down the flank and his cross being met by van Nistelrooy.

Solskjaer and Silvestre's addition to the United line-up had indeed made a vast difference, giving United the penetration they lacked without the injured Giggs, and it was the Norwegian who created the fourth, combining with Paul Scholes to set up Veron, who left footed the ball home from 30 yards out.

Solskjaer also set up United's fifth for Beckham, who scored from 15 yards, rounding off a memorable afternoon in North London.

When Tottenham manager Glen Hoddle was asked what had happened, his reply was only two words: 'half-time'. Before going on to say, 'Lord help us if they start keeping clean sheets as well.'

Sir Alex Ferguson, on the other hand, had plenty to say: 'In the first half we played as if we were feeling sorry for ourselves. You can either give in to that or do something about it and show your determination.

'They needed to rediscover what they are about. They are the best players in the country and they've got to play like it.

'Two things happened in the second half. We played with better width and we got a goal at the right time, straight after half-time.'

31

Newcastle United (A)

12 April 2003

'United lead way in £10m bid to sign Ronaldinho' proclaimed the Times *on the morning of United's journey to the North East to face Newcastle United, where a victory would give United a three-point advantage over second-placed Arsenal, if only for twenty-four hours, as the Gunners were not due to play until the Sunday.*

The twenty-three-year-old Brazilian, who it was reported would receive an initial £60,000 per week contract, would have made an excellent addition to the Old Trafford squad, but it was a transfer doomed to failure and one which still rankles with Sir Alex Ferguson to this day, although the performance up in the North East was to show that Manchester United did not require any South American flair and skills to gain notable victories and entertain the masses.

United had returned home from a midweek mauling in Madrid, losing 3-1 in the first leg of the Champions League quarter-final tie. The result, however, did little to daunt their search for yet another Premiership title, having trounced Liverpool 4-0 the previous Saturday. They were certainly on form on the domestic front, but with Newcastle enjoying a notable season under Sir Bobby Robson, sitting in third place, anything could happen.

Newcastle United: Given, Hughes, Woodgate, Bramble, Bernard, Solano, Dyer, Jenas (1), Robert, Shearer, Bellamy. Substitutes: Ameobi (1) for Solano, Viana for Robert and Lualua for Viana. Harper and Griffin not used.
United: Barthez, Brown, Ferdinand, Silvestre, O'Shea, Solskjaer (1), Keane, Butt, Scholes (3), Giggs (1), van Nistelrooy (1 pen.). Substitutes: Blanc for Brown, G. Neville for O'Shea and Forlan for Giggs. Ricardo and P. Neville not used.
Score: 6-2
Attendance: 52,164

'Never mind watching Real Madrid, this was like watching surreal Madrid,' wrote Andy Dunn in the *People*. 'It was as though Manchester United had returned from Spain infected with the bug of beautiful football – as though they had stolen the Madrid manual and spent three days cramming,' he continued, so impressed by the visitors' performance.

The game began somewhat controversially, with Shearer catching Keane with his elbow in a mid-air challenge after only three minutes. The England international put himself about even more four minutes later, when he caught Silvestre with a high challenge, bringing a few words, but nothing more, from the referee. A third, totally unnecessary, challenge on O'Shea in the twenty-second minute did, eventually, bring a booking for the Newcastle forward.

With the midweek defeat in Spain cast to the back of their minds, it was 'in the past so let's look to the future', but they were to receive something of a jolt in the twenty-first minute when Newcastle took the lead through Jenas.

Hughes crossed to Bellamy at the back post and the Welshman volley for goal from 8 yards out, which Barthez managed to beat away. As the United defence attempted to clear the ball, it only went as far as Jenas, whose 25-yard drive went zooming past a helpless Barthez, much to the joy of the home support.

The goal, however, was like a red rag to a bull, as it seemed to click a switch somewhere. United stormed into action and were 3-1 in front within seventeen minutes, with the goals coming in a devastating and frantic five-minute spell.

Prior to their goal, Newcastle had lost Robert with a leg injury, but it would not have made any difference had he remained in the thick of the action.

Van Nistelrooy saw a near-post effort blocked by Given, minutes after the home side had taken the lead; then two minutes over the half-hour, United equalised. Giggs' inch-perfect cross fell for Solskjaer who, having beaten the offside trap, controlled the ball with his chest before hooking the ball past Given.

Two minutes later, United were in front. The Newcastle defence was torn apart with a Scholes–Solskjaer one-two, the former accepting the return pass and hitting the ball first time past the advancing Given.

It was Scholes again in the thirty-seventh minute, making it 3-1 after Giggs waltzed through the Newcastle defence, cut in from the left, picked out Brown, who in turn passed to Scholes, who thundered the ball high into the top left-hand corner of the goal.

A minute prior to half-time, United scored a fourth. O'Shea beat Solano on the left, drifting past Hughes as he continued his run forward, before unleashing a powerful drive that smacked against the underside of the Newcastle crossbar. The effort deserved a goal in itself, but as the ball rebounded into play, it was Giggs, reacting quickest, who fired the ball home.

At 4-1 up, Giggs took no part in the second half with the visit of Real Madrid in mind, but he was rarely missed as United continued their assault on a Newcastle side, whose hopes of clinching their first championship since 1927 (they were in third place, six points behind United) were looking to be in tatters.

Forlan came on in place of Giggs, while O'Shea had to go off injured and was replaced by Gary Neville, the full-back getting quickly into the thick of the action and playing a part in United's fifth.

Scholes got the ball out to Solskjaer, who in turn sent Neville scurrying down the touchline. The full-back's cross, cut back across the face of the Newcastle goal, was missed by the defence and fell to Scholes at the back post to tap home for his hat-trick.

A sixth followed five minutes later, much to Newcastle's embarrassment. A clumsy late challenge by Bramble on Forlan resulted in a clear-cut penalty and from the spot-kick, and van Nistelrooy sent Given the wrong way for his thirty-sixth goal of the season. The Dutchman should have made it thirty-seven ten minutes from time, but his finish was too casual to beat Given.

United had taken their foot off the pedal a little in the second half and this allowed Newcastle to come into the game in brief flourishes. Shearer, quiet throughout, saw a shot blocked by Barthez, but the 'keeper's good work during in the preceding eighty-nine minutes was ruined when he made a complete hash of a kick out, which fell to Ameobi, who wasted no time in furthering the Frenchman's embarrassment with Newcastle's second.

'It's a great confidence boost,' said Sir Alex Ferguson. 'No question about that.'

'We played very well and created some good openings. It was a matter of being patient and when we got back into the game we played some fantastic football.

'When we were a goal down, we probably would have taken a point. We are very pleased to have won the way we did.

'We knew Arsenal's goal difference was five ahead before the game. Seven or eight wasn't beyond us today, but unfortunately it didn't happen.'

32

Real Madrid (H)

23 April 2003

After hitting Newcastle for six, United drew with title rivals Arsenal 2-2 and defeated Blackburn Rovers 3-1 to remain on top of the Premiership by one point, although the Gunners had a game in hand.

But all thoughts of yet another League title success were put on the back-burner, for a couple of days at least, as Real Madrid were due in town on a little matter of Champions League business, and although the Spaniards held a 3-1 advantage from the first leg, United and their supporters were confident that they could certainly score two at Old Trafford.

Madrid were, of course, synonymous with European football, and the European Cup/Champions League in particular, but Sir Alex Ferguson had got the better of them before and could certainly do so again.

'Given our record and history of scoring late in games, I'd always think we could score.

'It could be an advantage if it gets to that point of nothing happening with twenty minutes to go.

'Knowing our team, I wouldn't be disappointed if it was 0-0 after seventy minutes.

'Our form is probably the best of the season. We're playing good football and creating opportunities – that gives us a chance.

'I think we can score goals. The $64,000 question is if we can stop them scoring. That's the big test.'

There was also an added twist to the fixture, with Real confident of luring David Beckham to Madrid in the summer.

United: Barthez, O'Shea, Ferdinand, Brown, Silvestre, Veron, Butt, Keane, van Nistelrooy (1), Giggs, Solskjaer. Substitutes: Beckham (2) for Veron, P. Neville for Silvestre and Fortune for Keane. Ricardo, Blanc, Forlan and Fletcher not used.
Real Madrid: Casillas, Salgado, Hierro, Heluera (1 own goal), Roberto Carlos, Zidane, McManaman, Figo, Makelele, Ronaldo (3), Guti. Substitutes: Pavon for Figo, Portillo for McManaman and Solari for Ronaldo. Cesar, Flavio and Cambiasso not used.
Score: 4-3
Attendance: 66,708

Much of the prematch buzz surrounded the omission of David Beckham from the United starting line-up and Solskjaer being given a wide role. The United manager's decision to list Beckham among the substitutes gave the one-time United golden boy the opportunity to reflect on his future as he sat on the bench.

Old Trafford had enjoyed many memorable European nights; indeed, United's history is littered with them, going back to those pioneering days at Maine Road, and few who clicked through the turnstiles prior to kick-off realised that they were going to witness yet another notable occasion.

Many agreed that the selection of Solskjaer over Beckham was correct, given that the latter has never really enjoyed playing against Roberto Carlos. They were, however, rather mystified by the inclusion of Veron, as the midfielder had been out of action for some seven weeks with a knee injury. The manager was expecting perhaps just a little too much from the talented Argentinian.

United began well, van Nistelrooy drifting past Helguera and Roberto Carlos before forcing an early save from Casillas. Giggs also tested the Spanish 'keeper and John O'Shea surprised everyone by nutmegging Figo, but the danger was never far away.

Sure enough, with fourteen minutes gone, disaster struck.

Former Liverpool player Steve McManaman, booed on his every touch, even without the ball, played a pass forward for Zidane. The Frenchman moved in from the left before pushing the ball square to Guti. A quick look up and the ball flashed to Ronaldo, who left Ferdinand stranded before beating Barthez at his near post.

There was now a mountain to climb, one of Everest proportions, as United had to score three just to keep the tie alive.

Madrid came close again in the twenty-first minute, Figo scooping the ball into the night air and forcing Barthez to back-pedal to make the save.

United were a shadow of the team from recent games, with Veron failing to inspire from midfield. His only real involvement was a tackle on Makelele, which earned him a yellow card.

Giggs shot wide and Solskjaer forced a diving save from Casillas, but still United struggled and it was not until two minutes before the interval that they finally managed to claw themselves back into the game. Giggs threaded the ball to Solskjaer and the Norwegian managed to square the ball beyond the reach of Casillas to the lurking van Nistelrooy, who manoeuvred the ball home from a few yards out.

Could United turn the game on its head?

In first-half stoppage time, a goalmouth scramble almost brought a second, Casillas only just managing to kick a van Nistelrooy shot clear.

Expecting much more in the second half, the home support were eager for the game to restart, but within five minutes, they conceded a second.

Nicky Butt was left stranded by Zidane's 50-yard run, the ball being moved on to Figo. The Spaniard's chip towards goal rebounded off the far post and was not properly cleared by the United defence. It was snatched upon by Roberto Carlos and he pulled the ball back towards his fellow Brazilian, with Ronaldo side-footing the ball home for his second. It was a killer goal, more or less confirming that the game was now over as a contest, leaving United to score four in forty minutes. Not impossible, but...

A chink of light appeared almost immediately, as Helguera, in a panic, turned a shot from Veron past Casillas, then Solskjaer and Veron both saw shots saved by the Madrid 'keeper as United refused to lie down.

Almost on the hour, Madrid scored a third, Figo the supplier and that man Ronaldo the scorer, beating Wes Brown with ease before unleashing a stunning drive from 25 yards out.

In the sixty-third minute, the United manager threw Beckham into the fray, replacing the ineffective Veron, and he immediately looked as though he had something to prove, but his welcome into the action was nothing like the noise that echoed around the stadium four minutes later, when Ronaldo was substituted, as the crowd rose as one to salute a remarkable individual performance from a player who had been booed off the pitch at the Bernabeu in the first leg.

Beckham whipped in one of his trademark crosses, and Solskjaer should have done better with a diving header, then with nineteen minutes remaining the United substitute scored with a stunning free-kick, going on to notch a second five minutes from time, sliding in at the far post, stirring the game into a frantic finale.

But there was no way back, and although United claimed a victory on the night, they were well beaten over the two legs.

'My prediction of the match was a bit unfortunate for me,' said Sir Alex Ferguson, 'because I knew if we could keep them out we had a marvellous chance – but we couldn't keep them out.

'I was proud of the effort our players put in. From a footballing point of view we have seen a game that kept within the traditions that both teams have of wanting to win matches. And because of the way both teams play there were an enormous amount of chances in the match.

'When you score four goals at home you expect to win – but you can't legislate for someone like Ronaldo.

'Maybe the key moment was just after half-time when Seba Veron hit a volley that struck their goalkeeper on the chest. If that had gone in I don't know how the game would have gone.

'Not until they scored did we come alive, but the end product from Manchester United was far superior in terms of the number of chances we made in the match.

'Iker Casillas made goodness knows how many stops, so I don't feel it was an unfair result.'

33

Bolton Wanderers (H)

16 August 2003

The sports pages of Wednesday 13 August carried news of Manchester United's latest acquisition, hailing him as 'David Beckham Mark 2' – quite a title for Cristiano Ronaldo, a £12.24-million signing from Sporting Lisbon, making him the second most expensive teenager in football history.

The eighteen-year-old Portuguese star, given the iconic No. 7 shirt, had been on United's radar since breaking into the Sporting side the previous year and, thanks to the club's close connections with the Lisbon club, an agreement was in place a few months previously.

'When I saw Manchester United play on television a few years back, I never thought that someday I would be here (in Manchester), and so soon, even though I dreamed of it,' said Ronaldo.

'Cristiano is one of the most exciting young players I have ever seen,' proclaimed Sir Alex Ferguson upon sealing the player's signature.

'After we played Sporting last week, the lads in the dressing room talked about him constantly on the plane back from the game, they urged me to sign him. That's how highly they rated him.

'He is an extremely talented footballer, a two-footed attacker who can play anywhere up front.'

United: Howard, P. Neville, Ferdinand, Silvestre, Fortune, Solskjaer, Keane, Butt, Giggs (2), Scholes (1), van Nistelrooy (1). Substitutes: Ronaldo for Butt, Djemba-Djemba for Solskjaer and Forlan for Giggs. Carroll and O'Shea not used.
Bolton Wanderers: Jaaskelainen, Hunt, Laville, N'Gotty, Gardner, Glannakopoulos, Okocha, Campo, Nolan, Pedersen, Davies. Substitutes: Facey for Glannakopoulos, Frandsen for Nolan and Djokaeff for Pedersen. Poole and Barness not used.
Score: 4-0
Attendance: 67,647

Bolton had been prewarned about United's new signing prior to the short journey to Manchester for the opening fixture of the new season, thanks to their Brazilian striker, Jardel. On the eve of the match, manager Sam Allerdyce revealed, 'Jardel tells me he is an unbelievable, fantastic footballer. Who knows how long it will take to get him ready for the Premiership or if he'll be introduced tomorrow.'

As it turned out, the latest signing had to be content with a place on the bench, as United began their defence of the title.

United began brightly, Scholes and van Nistelrooy both prominent in the early attacks, but the home side were well aware of allowing their visitors too much of the ball, as they had won on their previous two trips to Old Trafford.

With six minutes gone, Nicky Butt played a quick ball in to Scholes, who moved towards the Bolton by line before crossing. The ball, however, went behind both van Nistelrooy and Solskjaer and was scrambled to safety by the Bolton defence.

Three minutes later, it was Keane surging forward from yet another Scholes pass and the ball was threaded wide to Solskjaer. Jaaskelainen advanced from his goal as the Norwegian shot and managed to tip the ball over the bar.

Jay-Jay Okocha threatened the United defence from time to time, with Kevin Nolan wasting ideal opportunities to give the visitors the lead. One effort was tipped over by Howard; another, when completely unmarked in the United penalty area, was fortunately blocked by a United defender.

Defensively, however, United were poor, with Keane working overtime to keep Bolton at bay, but ten minutes before the break, United got the break they needed. Solskjaer was dragged down by N'Gotty, and from this free-kick, Giggs curled the ball wide of Jaaskelainen, the ball going in off the post.

Just before the interval, Nolan went close yet again, but after a few well-chosen words from the manager at half-time, it was a completely different United who emerged for the second half.

A volley from Keane after dispossessing Campo went narrowly over, but United continued to struggle. That was, until the introduction of Ronaldo on the hour mark, replacing Nicky Butt.

Off the bench for a mere ten minutes and he had already humiliated two Bolton defenders before Nolan took offence to being taunted by the young upstart and brought him down inside the area. Unfortunately, the incident failed to produce a goal, as van Nistelrooy's spot-kick was saved by Jaaskelainen, who palmed the ball wide.

The 'keeper, however, was to blot his copybook sixteen minutes from time when, having caused mayhem down the left, Ronaldo crossed to Scholes at the back post, who volleyed straight at the Bolton 'keeper. Such was the power, he failed to hold van Nistelrooy's shot, allowing Giggs to claim his second of the match.

Every time Ronaldo received the ball, the crowd were on the edge of their seats wondering what the youngster was going to do next. Step-overs had the crowd mesmerised, never mind the Bolton defenders. His silver boots shone in the afternoon sun.

Bolton continued to press forward, but this played right into United's hands. Djemba-Djemba, having replaced Solskjaer, played Scholes through and, as Bolton looked for offside, he went round Jaaskelainen to put United three in front.

A Ronaldo cross should have been converted by van Nistelrooy, but the Dutchman headed wide, although with only three minutes remaining he made amends, latching onto a Forlan pass to score the fourth.

As the full-time whistle blew, the name of Ronaldo echoed around the ground. It was now a case of 'David who?' Old Trafford had not witnessed such a mesmeric display of skill since the halcyon days of George Best.

In the *Daily Mirror*, Oliver Holt wrote, 'It was supposed to be more about what Manchester United had lost rather than what they had gained.

'The end of a summer spent digesting the loss of David Beckham and mulling over the departure of Juan Sebastian Veron.

'How strange, then, that ninety minutes later we all left feeling we had been privileged to witness the birth of a bright, shining star.

'In half an hour of a spellbinding debut, new £12-million signing Cristiano Ronaldo made you feel anything was possible in the Theatre of Dreams again this season.

'The performance of the kid wearing Beckham's old number seven on his back raged through the crowd like a power surge and sent them home dreaming that maybe they had caught their first glimpse of a player who will become a legend.

'Not just a new number seven, but someone who might even have the skill to be better than Beckham. Who might be the cornerstone of a new dynasty.

'They saw a kid who can cross with both feet, someone who can bamboozle a defender with a step-over, a drag-back or a jink from a bag full of tricks. Someone with pace. Someone who, even though he is only eighteen, seems to know when to release the ball. Someone who wants to destroy, not over indulge.

'A kid who, half an hour after the game, was already being compared to George Best, Eric Cantona and Ryan Giggs in his first flush of youth.'

Manager Sir Alex Ferguson could not have been happier with his new arrival. 'It was a marvellous debut. Unbelievable. But he is only a boy and we have to remember that. We need to be careful with him.

'The thing that pleased me most was Cristiano took a bad tackle and got straight back up – that told me something about him.

'You just have to look at the crucial contribution he made after he came on. He won a penalty and sent the cross in for their second goal. He was different class.'

34

Fenerbahce (H)

28 September 2004

'Roonmania is gripping Old Trafford, with even Sir Alex Ferguson and United's biggest names excited by the prospect of £29m Wayne Rooney's debut,' penned Stuart Mathieson in the Manchester Evening News sports section on Monday 27 September.

Twenty-nine days after his record-breaking £29-million move from Everton, the eighteen-year-old was preparing to play some part in United's Champions League fixture against Fenerbahce, having fully recovered from the broken foot sustained in Portugal during Euro 2004.

'He could do with a reserve game first,' said the United manager, 'but the boy is chomping at the bit now. He is desperate to start his career at United. I am desperate to see him, I must admit, and the players are too.'

Forty-eight hours later, the former Evertonian again claimed the headlines on not just the local sports pages, but also the national ones. 'Rooney goes on the rampage to launch Old Trafford love affair' filled the back page of the Independent. The report regaled their readers with how the baby-faced youngster demolished the Turkish champions on his own, notching a memorable hat-trick in United's 6-2 victory.

United: Carroll, G. Neville, Heinze, Ferdinand, Silvestre, Bellion (1), Djemba-Djemba, Kleberson, Giggs (1), Rooney (3), van Nistelrooy (1). Substitutes: Fletcher for Giggs, Miller for van Nistelrooy and P. Neville for Heinze. Ricardo, Ronaldo, Smith and O'Shea not used.
Fenerbahce: Recber, Baris, Lucanio, Umit, Fatih, Balci, Marco Aurelio, Nobre (1), Sanli (1), Alex, van Hooijdonk. Substitutes: Serhat for Faith. Demirel, Fabiano, Lima, Yozgatli, Hacioglu, Turaci and Sahin not used.
Score: 6-2
Attendance: 67,128

With Keane and Ronaldo rested, the United manager went for the unlikely midfield partnership of Kleberson and Djemba-Djemba, and it took the former only seven minutes to make his mark, winning the ball and breaking down the left, his cross finding the head of Ryan Giggs, who planted the ball in the bottom right-hand corner of the net.

Ten minutes later, Wayne Rooney stepped into the spotlight.

Running onto a through ball from van Nistelrooy, and without breaking stride, he unleashed a powerful shot into the roof of the Fenerbahce net, having come close only minutes earlier with an equally thunderous shot that flew narrowly over.

The visitors thought they had pulled a goal back when van Hooijdonk headed home an Alex corner, but the ball was judged to have gone out of play and they were soon to fall further behind in the twenty-eighth minute when, taking a short pass from Giggs, Rooney unleashed a right-footed drive, from almost 30 yards out, into the bottom left-hand corner.

A tussle between van Nistelrooy and Aurelio reignited the tie that, up until now, was more or less a foregone conclusion thanks to the debutant. Then, two minutes into the second half, the Turks pulled a goal back, Nobre tapping home a corner with the United defence in a generous mood.

But the Croxteth kid was far from finished. Every time he touched the ball there was a sense of panic in the opposition's defence and a hint of growing confidence from the player himself.

Ten minutes into the second half, Roy Carroll launched the ball forward from a goal kick and, as it neared the opposition penalty area, van Nistelrooy was held back by Luciano. Although he was still something of a novice, a newcomer to the side, Rooney wasted little time in letting his teammates know that he was taking the kick.

Full of confidence, the ball was curled past the luckless Recber.

To their credit, Fenerbahce didn't give up and caused the United defence problems from set pieces. From a corner, given away by Rooney, Baris forced Carroll into making a point-blank save, but the United 'keeper failed to hold the ball and Sanli was on hand to drive the ball home and put the visitors back into the game.

Their revival, however, was short-lived. Fletcher replaced Giggs just after the hour mark to add an extra body in midfield and, sixteen minutes after coming on, the Scot picked out van Nistelrooy with a long pass and the Dutchman, shaking off a couple of challenges, extended United's lead.

With nine minutes remaining, Rooney, still very much involved in the flow of the game, headed the ball goalwards and Bellion scored United's sixth.

Few could have imagined that Rooney's introduction into the Manchester United story would have conjured up a chapter all to itself; even the Turkish press devoted countless lines to the 'magician' and 'that hormonal child, who if he were a Turkish citizen would not even have been allowed to do military service because he is too fat'.

He might miss out on national service in Turkey, but in Manchester, his call-up into the United front line was certainly going to be an ongoing occurrence, with his manager saying, 'It's a great start for him. He is only eighteen and a young boy, don't forget.

'He obviously tired in the last twenty minutes but, given that it was his first game since the European Championships, you could expect that. I think he can only get stronger.

'The important thing for me as a coach is to allow the boy to develop naturally without too much public attention. I want him to be as ordinary as he can.'

35

Wigan Athletic (N)

26 February 2006

It was only February, a time when Manchester United's trophy assault was normally only beginning to warm up. The finishing line and the winner's podium were still on the distant horizon, but the silverware was firmly targeted and the hunger was there to succeed.

But February 2006 was different, very different, as United were out of the Premiership race, a dozen points adrift of leaders Chelsea; out of the Champions League, finishing bottom of their group, having scored a meagre three goals in their six games, the first time they had failed to progress beyond the group stages for eleven years; out of the FA Cup, beaten by arch-rivals Liverpool and a solitary Peter Crouch goal.

There was, however, a fourth competition – the Carling Cup, a competition considered by many, United included, as little more than an introductory tournament for promising youngsters.

The fourth-round tie against West Bromwich Albion was played against a backdrop of tears and emotion, following the death of George Best five days previously. The Irishman had made his debut against the Midlands side back in September 1963, but as the competition progressed, it was the senior members of the United squad who nudged the team towards the final in Cardiff and their first trophy success since the FA Cup triumph in 2004.

It had been too long for a club of United's stature to go without a trophy.

Success was also important for the United manager, not simply because it had been a while without, but this particular final was coming at a time when the doubters were once again voicing their opinions, hinting that perhaps this would indeed be Ferguson's final season in charge, with his one-year rolling contract making it easy for the Glazer family, who had taken over ownership of the club less than a year previously, to make changes at the top.

United: Van der Sar, Brown, Silvestre, Ferdinand, G. Neville, O'Shea, Park, Giggs, Ronaldo (1), Saha (1), Rooney (2). Substitutes: Richardson for Ronaldo, Evra for Silvestre and Vidic for Brown. Van Nistelrooy and Howard not used.
Wigan Athletic: Pollitt, Chimbonda, Henchoz, De Zeeuw, Baines, Teale, Bullard, Kavanagh, Scharner, Roberts, Camara. Substitutes: McCulloch for Henchoz, Ziegler for Kavanagh and Filan for Pollitt. Jackson and Johansson not used.

Score: 4-0
Attendance: 66,866

The FA Cup defeat at Liverpool had robbed United of the services of Alan Smith, a broken leg and a dislocated ankle effectively ending not simply his season but his career. Gabriel Heinze was also missing due to cruciate ligament damage, as was Paul Scholes with an eye injury. Sir Alex Ferguson, however, had enough resources to call upon and ensure success against Wigan Athletic.

Backed by an enthusiastic support, making the best of the occasion, Wigan set the early pace of the game, Teale drifting effortlessly past Silvestre down the wing in the third minute, with his finely measured cross finding the head of Camara, nipping in front of Wes Brown, but the ball went over, rather than under the United bar.

An ideal start for the underdogs, but a minute later former United youngster Mike Pollitt, in the Wigan goal, pulled a hamstring while collecting a pass back, and he was forced to leave the field ten minutes later. Before making his way to the touchline, he had watched in relief as Rooney's header from a Gary Neville cross had hammered against his crossbar.

With seventeen minutes gone, United should have taken the lead. Rooney brushed past a couple of Wigan defenders in a 50-yard dash for goal, cutting the ball back into the path of Ronaldo, but the Portuguese winger completely missed the ball.

Bullard tested van der Sar from 30 yards in the nineteenth minute, but it was United who were to strike the first blow in the thirty-second minute. Saha flicked the ball on and the failure of both Chimbonda and Henchoz to intercept allowed Rooney to run through and score. Six minutes later, Rooney should have made it two. Playing a one-two with Ryan Giggs, the final ball was just a fraction too high to guide the ball goalwards.

Wigan began the second half strongly, almost snatching an equaliser when Camara, with his back to goal, turned Ferdinand inside the box, but was disappointed to see his shot stopped by the legs of van der Sar.

But, as a contest, it was soon all over. Substitute Filan saved brilliantly from Saha following a Giggs, Ronaldo, Neville move, but failed to hold the ball and the former Fulham player reacted quickly to score United's second.

In another Wigan attack, Teal crossed towards Roberts, but van der Sar managed to knock it over the bar. Then, on the hour, United added a third. Henchoz made a mess of a clearance, sending it to the feet of Saha. 40 yards from goal, he picked out Ronaldo with a finely measured pass and the ball was despatched into the corner of the net.

A fourth followed a few minutes later, courtesy of Rooney. Giggs crossed into the area, Chimbonda headed the ball up in the air, and Ferdinand then headed the ball down to the feet of Rooney, who swept the ball home from close range. The opportunity for the same player to claim a hat-trick was scorned when he was through on goal but chipped the ball into the side netting.

Wigan, to their credit, tried their hardest, but were no match for a flamboyant United, who almost threatened to score with every attack and although they continued to press towards the United goal until the end, there was to be no consolation goal.

Prior to the presentation of the trophy, the United players donned T-shirts bearing the legend 'For you Smudge', in a tribute to the injured Alan Smith.

As the United players celebrated with the trophy in front of their supporters, a stone-faced Ruud van Nistelrooy, who had been an unnamed substitute, failed to join in the celebrations and left the pitch before his teammates. It was to be the beginning of the end for the Dutch striker and United.

Speaking about the striker, his manager said, 'I explained to Ruud that Louis Saha deserved to play because he'd already scored five goals in the competition.'

As for his team performance, 'In 1992 when we won the competition, it began a good spell for us and, hopefully, this can be the same again. Our attacking play was excellent.'

36

Roma (H)

10 April 2007

Manchester United has a rich European history; far more than those European Cup/ Champions League and European Cup Winners' Cup successes conjure up, with memorable nights in the likes of Madrid, Lisbon and Turin, and equally unforgettable ones much nearer to home at Maine Road.

But right up alongside them all are the ninety minutes of Tuesday 10 April 2007.

Drawn against Roma in the quarter-final of the Champions League, the first leg saw United beaten by the odd goal in the Olympic Stadium, in a game overshadowed by violence inside and outside the ground, and the United section of the stadium attacked by baton-welding police following the Italians first goal. To compound matters, United had Paul Scholes sent off for two yellow cards in the thirty-fourth minute.

The defeat left United with a lot to do, despite the 'away' goal, although the United manager was confident that his side could progress. 'We always recover, we cover well. I think we are in a good position for this game. I'm pleased that we managed a goal with ten men and when we did, Roma became nervous for a period.

'I think we will create chances but in my experience of Europe we have missed a lot of chances, particularly in two semi-finals here, if we can take them this time, we'll have a massive chance.'

United: Van der Sar, Brown, Ferdinand, Heinze, O'Shea, Ronaldo (2), Fletcher, Carrick (2), Giggs, Rooney (1), Smith (1). Substitutes: Evra (1) for O'Shea, Richardson for Carrick and Solskjaer for Giggs. Dong, Cathcart, Eagles and Kuszczak not used.
Roma: Doni, Panucci, Mexes, Chivu, Cassetti, Wilhelmsson, De Rossi (1), Vucinic, Pizarro, Mancini, Totti. Substitutes: Rosi for Wilhelmsson, Faty for De Rossi and Okaka Chuka for Mancini. Curci, Defendi, Ferrari and Taddei not used.
Score: 7-1
Attendance: 74, 476

The atmosphere bubbled away outside the ground in the hours before the game, with some nasty scenes close to the stadium as tensions ran high following the problems in Rome the previous week. But by the time the stadium was full and the referee blew his whistle to start the game, the only revenge sought was for a United victory.

Sir Alex Ferguson gambled with Solskjaer on the bench and Alan Smith in his starting line-up, the latter having yet to regain his old form since the horror injury at Anfield over a year ago.

The opening ten minutes belonged to Roma, the Italians showing everyone that they were capable of grabbing what could well be a vital away goal, but as the crowd got behind United, play switched into the opposite half of the field, where it was to remain for most of the game.

There were only thirteen minutes on the clock when Ronaldo took the ball inside before passing to Carrick, who took one touch before firing home with a swerving drive from 25 yards, leaving the Roma 'keeper stranded.

Five minutes later, Heinze advanced down the left and, in a series of one-touch passes, Carrick and Rooney picked out Giggs in the middle. Chivu failed to cut out the Welshman's through ball and it fell to Smith to tuck the ball home for his first goal since November 2005.

Old Trafford erupted. United had nosed themselves in front on aggregate and by the twentieth minute they were three in front on the night. Smith passed to Giggs who, beating the Roma offside trap, centred towards goal, where Rooney evaded three Italian defenders, diverting the ball home off the far post.

Carrick missed a sitter but a minute before the interval it was 4-0. Ronaldo advanced down the right for the umpteenth time and fired home from the edge of the area. That semi-final place was all but secured.

Many expected United to ease up slightly in the second half, although keeping a tight hold of the game, but three minutes after the restart, it was game, set and match when Ronaldo took advantage of the rather hesitant Roma defence, prodding home after a Giggs corner was only partly cleared. When the ball was returned to him from Rooney, he crossed low into the Roma area where Ronaldo scored from 3 yards out.

Carrick scored his second of the night on the hour, with a shot into the top corner, and when Roma managed to pull a goal back in the sixty-ninth minute through De Rossi, but it mattered little.

Nine minutes from time, Evra, on as substitute for O'Shea, rounded off the scoring with another long-range drive for United's seventh.

It was a night that saw records tumble: the biggest victory in the European Cup/ Champions League since Real Madrid beat Seville 8-0 way back in 1958; the biggest winning margin in a Champions League knock-out tie; United's biggest win since their 7-1 win over Waterford in 1968.

For manager Sir Alex Ferguson, he claimed it was his 'greatest night at Old Trafford'.

'You never expect a scoreline like that. The quality of our game was so high that once we scored the second and third goals I was in the dugout thinking, "This could be something really big here." But even so, I wasn't expecting that.

'It was a special night and hopefully not a one-off in terms of the quality, but certainly the number of goals and the quality of play was very, very high.

'We have to win something to be seen as a great team and hopefully we will do that now. The way they (the players) are playing and enjoying their football, they deserve it.'

The victory had placed United in the semi-final of the Champions League, while they were also in the semi-final of the FA Cup and sitting three points ahead of Chelsea in the Premiership.

As it turned out, there was to be no repeat of the 1999 treble-winning season. Instead they had to be content with their ninth League title, their first since 2003, while in the Champions League, having beaten Milan 3-2 in the Old Trafford first leg, they were to lose the return 3-0.

In the FA Cup, it was runners-up medals at the new Wembley, after losing 1-0 to Chelsea after extra time.

37

Everton (A)
28 April 2007

Middlesbrough held United to a 1-1 draw at Old Trafford on 21 April, Mark Viduka's forty-fifth-minute headed goal blowing the title race wide open, although twenty-four hours later, with Chelsea having also dropped a point against another North East club, Newcastle, things were not as bad as they had been.

United still sat at the top, three points clear of the Stamford Bridge club, with only four games remaining and both teams having to face each other in what could be a championship decider in the penultimate fixture of the season.

They were also still involved in the Champions League, with a semi-final tie against AC Milan next up before the next domestic League fixture against Everton, while the possibility of yet another treble loomed on the horizon, as an FA Cup final place had already been secured thanks to a 4-1 semi-final victory over Watford. Title-chasing rivals Chelsea were their final opponents.

In that Champions League fixture, a narrow 3-2 win against the Italians gave United a slender lead, but thoughts of a place in the Champions League final had to be put on hold, as the visit to Goodison Park took immediate priority.

Everton: Turner, Hibbert, Yobo, Arteta, Stubbs (1), Lescott, Neville (1 own goal), Osman, Vaughan, Carsley, Fernandes (1). Substitutes: McFadden for Osman, Beattie for Vaughan and van der Meyde for Carsley. Wright and Naysmith not used.
United: Van der Sar, O'Shea (1), Brown, Heinze, Evra, Solskjaer, Carrick, Scholes, Giggs, Rooney (1), Smith. Substitutes: Richardson for Evra, Ronaldo for Smith and Eagles (1) for Solskjaer. Kuszczak and Lee not used.
Score: 4-2
Attendance: 39,682

'Now is the time to be great' was Sir Alex Ferguson's rallying cry prior to the trip along the East Lancs Road. 'Now we focus on the Premiership again, knowing that we are involved in yet another match of immense significance. Every match feels like a cup final now. I wouldn't have it any other way because this is what it's all about, big games on the last lap of the season.'

Everton, with not the best of records against United, opened strongly with the visitor's defence failing to handle the attacking threats of Vaughan and Osman, along with the midfield prowess of Michael Arteta. Their early determination earned them a well-deserved lead after twelve minutes.

Patrice Evra tripped Arteta some 35 yards out and, suspecting little danger, van der Sar requested a defensive wall of only two. Stubbs hammered the ball towards goal and as it passed the 6-yard line, Carrick stuck out his leg and the ball deflected off it, leaving van der Sar helpless as it flew past him into the net.

United continued to stutter along through the remainder of the first half and Everton could have considered themselves unlucky to go in at the break only one goal in front. Their midfield were clearly outshining their United counterparts. As for the visitors, they were too hurried in their play, with Rooney, the ex-Evertonian, alone up front, their only real threat at goal. One effort almost caught out Turner in the Everton goal as it flew through the legs of Hibbert, while he was only inches away from connecting with a Giggs volley, which flew across the face of the Everton goal.

United's title hopes were beginning to look fragile, as news filtered through that Chelsea were leading 2-1 against Bolton Wanderers at home.

Bolton, however, managed to draw level, but it was to matter little, for now, as United soon found themselves in further trouble.

Five minutes into the second half, Everton made it 2-0. Evra allowed Arteta too much room and the ball was laid forward towards Fernandes. Carrick and Brown were too slow to react and the Everton man quickly moved the ball onto his right foot before driving it firmly past van der Sar from 20 yards.

The United support were now becoming more than a little frustrated, mainly due to the fact that Ronaldo, their talisman, remained on the bench. An injury in training had forced him to be omitted from the starting line-up.

With the pressure mounting on United, Everton surprisingly began to crack.

Eleven minutes after going 2-0 in front, United won a corner and the ball was floated into the penalty area by Giggs. Stand-in 'keeper Turner, playing because first-choice Tim Howard, under the terms of his transfer from United, was not allowed to play, dropped the ball with no one near him and a grateful John O'Shea powered the ball home.

Ronaldo was quickly introduced to the fray. Immediately, Everton sensed trouble, and seven minutes later United were level.

Turner, not wishing to make the same mistake twice, remained static as Carrick sent over another corner. Up jumped Ronaldo to head towards goal and as former United player Phil Neville attempted to clear amid a goalmouth scramble, he could only manage to turn the ball into his own net.

With eleven minutes remaining, United took the lead for the first time and, much to the annoyance of the home support, the goal came from Wayne Rooney.

As concentration within the Everton ranks wavered, Hibbert passed the ball across the face of his own 18-yard box, and it was pounced upon by Ronaldo, who immediately found O'Shea out wide. The Irishman's cross came off an Everton defender to the feet of Rooney, who calmly side-footed the ball past Turner.

As the game reached its finale, the final score from Stamford Bridge revealed that Chelsea had been held 2-2. United, unlike many other teams who would have settled to be a goal in front in such an important fixture with only minutes remaining, were not finished yet and could have been 5-2 in front before United did add a fourth.

Ronaldo, looking up and seeing young substitute Chris Eagles running forward and into space, hit the ball forward. Eagles almost stumbled as he gathered the ball on the edge of the Everton area, but managed to keep his feet and take a couple of steps to his right before curling the ball wide of the out stretched arm of Turner to clinch an important victory, with his first senior goal for the club.

'I can't explain the game,' the United manager admitted. 'Everton scored two goals from two great strikes and at that point I was toying with sending on Cristiano Ronaldo.

'I thought I would if we got a goal back, even though he is carrying an injury.

'We then got a break when their 'keeper dropped the ball.

'I knew the focus would be on Ronaldo and that would suit us because we also have Ryan Giggs, Paul Scholes and Rooney.

'I would say that it was meant to be.'

38

Chelsea (N)

21 May 2008

Manchester United's Champions League legacy should, in reality, have been much richer, and at least two other final appearances, in addition to their two memorable triumphs, should appear in their list of honours.

Failure at the semi-final stage of any competition is hard to take, and their defeat at the hands of Milan, one step away from the Champions League final in 2007, was indeed difficult to take. But twelve months down the line, that disappointment was erased when United faced Barcelona in the 2008 semi-final.

Drawing the first leg in Spain 0-0, a solitary Paul Scholes was enough to take United through to the final in Moscow, an all-Premiership affair with Chelsea supplying the opposition.

'People ask whether our players have the experience to take opportunities like this one before them,' said Sir Alex Ferguson as his team prepared for the final. 'But young people aren't afraid. That's the great quality young people have.

'When I was a kid, I used to climb church steeples looking for pigeons, go under bridges and all the rest of it. Now, if I look outside a window more than two stories high, I get vertigo.

'That's what age does to you. When you are young you are fearless, you don't have that. So hopefully the younger ones in our team will have no fear in Moscow.'

Busby's Babes were fearless and, in the final fixture of a season that marked the fiftieth anniversary of the disaster at Munich, the opportunity was there to pay tribute to that wonderful team that was never given the opportunity to fulfil its true potential.

United: Van der Sar, Brown, Ferdinand, Vidic, Evra, Hargreaves (1 pen.), Scholes, Carrick (1 pen.), Ronaldo (1), Tevez (1 pen.), Rooney. Substitutes: Giggs (1 pen.) for Scholes, Nani (1 pen.) for Rooney and Anderson (1 pen.) for Brown. Kuszczak, O'Shea, Fletcher and Silvestre not used.
Chelsea: Cech, Essien, Carvalho, Terry, A. Cole (1 pen.), Ballack (1 pen.), Makelele, Lampard (1 and 1 pen.), J. Cole, Drogba, Malouda. Substitutes: Belletti (1 pen.) for Makelele, Anelka for J. Cole and Kalou (1 pen.) for Malouda. Cuicini, Shevchenko, Obi and Alex not used.
Score: 1-1 (6-5 penalties)
Attendance: 69,552

A red army of some 30,000 United supporters flocked to Moscow's Luzhniki Stadium on an evening of unrelenting rain, but there was nothing that was going to dampen their spirits as they got behind their team, not wishing to suffer the taunts of the Stamford Bridge support in the forthcoming meetings between the two sides on the domestic stage.

The early stages of the game were something of a cat-and-mouse affair, dull and uninspiring, although United could consider themselves unfortunate not to be ahead after Ronaldo's cross was intercepted by Terry when it dropped towards the head of Rooney. It wasn't until the twenty-second minute, when Scholes ended up with a bloodied nose following a challenge on Makelele – both players earning a yellow card – that the game seemed to spring into life.

Returning to the fray after attention on the touchline, the United midfielder, along with Wes Brown, engineered the move that was to produce the opening goal in the twenty-sixth minute. As Rooney moved towards the Chelsea near post, Tevez darted inside, pulling Chelsea defenders with them, and as Brown's cross dropped, Essien was left static as Ronaldo leaped high into the air to head firmly past Cech from 10 yards out. It was his forty-second goal of the season.

The goal left Chelsea with little option but to adopt a more attacking formation, offering some excitement to the neutral observers, and one of several attacks almost led to the equaliser, when Drogba headed Lampard's cross back towards Ballack, forcing Ferdinand to head the ball towards his own goal. Van der Sar managed to claw the goalbound shot away to safety.

At the opposite end, eleven minutes before half-time, Cech was soon to save Chelsea from going further behind. Rooney picked up the ball in his own half and, spotting Ronaldo breaking down the left, he unleashed a pinpoint pass. Ronaldo in turn crossed the ball into the Chelsea area, where Tevez brought the best out of the Chelsea 'keeper with a stopping header.

Unable to hold the ball, Terry attempted to clear, but the ball went only as far as Carrick, who met the ball full-on. However, Cech was again equal to the effort, palming the ball away to safety.

It was now almost end-to-end stuff.

Tevez slid in but just failed to convert a Rooney cross, while Ferdinand was booked for a block on Lampard, with Ballack's free-kick flying over the United bar. But with the referee checking his watch as half-time approached, disaster struck.

A Ferdinand clearance was intercepted by Lampard, who picked out Essien. His powerful return shot struck both Vidic and Ferdinand before landing at the feet of Lampard, who kept his composure before lifting the ball over the diving van der Sar.

It was a harsh blow for United and allowed Chelsea back into the game. As the second half got underway, they appeared to have the bit between their teeth, with Lampard and Makelele running the midfield.

Tevez and Makelele tussled in midfield, while Drogba hit the post from 30 yards. Ferguson replaced Scholes with Giggs, with three minutes of normal time remaining, the Welshman breaking Sir Bobby Charlton's appearance record of 758. Then, in the last minute, Rio Ferdinand breathed a sigh of relief when a somewhat heavy challenge on Joe Cole was ignored by the referee.

And so into extra time.

With only four minutes of the additional thirty played, Lampard hit the United bar from just inside the penalty area, after good work from Cole and Ballack, as both teams edging towards that crucial next goal.

Six minutes later, Terry was forced to head a Giggs effort over his own crossbar after Evra had pushed forward and cut the ball back to his teammate.

The game's pivotal moment arrived in the 116th minute. Due to an injury stoppage, with the ball out of play for a throw-in, Tevez, having been thrown the ball to restart play, decided that instead of kicking it back to Cech, he would kick the ball back out of play, much to the annoyance of the Chelsea players.

Much pushing and shoving followed and, as Vidic moved in to protect the Argentinian, Drogba, who had been involved in a tussle with the United defender six minutes earlier, slapped him across the face in full view of the referee, leaving the official with no alternative but to send the Chelsea player off. Both Tevez and Ballack, who were involved in the original incident, were booked.

But despite the efforts of both teams, there was no further scoring and so it was down to penalty kicks.

Chelsea were already at a disadvantage without their regular spot-kick taker in Drogba and they went one behind when Tevez, the man behind his dismissal, slotted home the first.

Ballack levelled the scoring with a powerful kick, and then Carrick edged United in front again, his kick going high into the Chelsea net. Belletti stroked the ball to the bottom right of van der Sar's goal, but suddenly the advantage went Chelsea's way, as Ronaldo stood in anguish as his spot-kick was saved by Cech.

Van der Sar managed to get his hand to Lampard's kick, but failed to stop it. Hargreaves blasted his effort past Cech. Cole then made it 4-3 to the Londoners as the pressure continued to rise.

Nani made it 4-4, but it could have mattered little, as a goal from Chelsea's final kick would give them the trophy.

Forward strode John Terry, and in the United end a feeling of foreboding filled the air, but this was short-lived, as when he kicked the ball he slipped and it flew past van der Sar's post.

It was all square.

Anderson, a rare goalscorer for United, showed tremendous calm and made no mistake with a shot down the middle. Kalou hit his kick high into the top right-hand corner as it began to look like the two 'keepers would have the deciding kicks.

Next up for United was Ryan Giggs, who calmly stroked the ball home. His confidence, however, was not shared by Nicolas Anelka, who looked far from happy as he placed the ball on the spot. His face looked drained of emotion seconds later as his kick, to van der Sar's right, was palmed away by the Dutchman.

It was 1.34 a.m. in Moscow. The game had begun the day before, but there was still a lot of celebrating to do before anyone of a red persuasion would think about going to bed.

United were, once again, Champions of Europe.

'This is the first penalty shoot-out I have won in a big game,' exclaimed the delighted United manager. 'I've won the Community Shield on penalties, but FA Cups, Scottish Cups – never. I'm so proud of my players and I think they have the makings of my best-ever team. This is a fantastic achievement and we deserved it.'

39

Liga de Quito (N)

21 December 2008

As Champions of Europe, United had the opportunity to go one step further and claim the title – Champions of the World – and thankfully the World Club Championship fixture had come a long way from the trouble-strewn, two-legged affair of the sixties, when both United and Glasgow Celtic became involved in games that were little more than stop-start affairs, involving countless petty fouls and more serious unsavoury incidents against Estudiantes and Racing Club respectively.

The present-day competition had moved away from its South American–European roots and now took place in more peaceful climates, with United heading to Yokohama, where they were to compete in a four-club tournament involving Japanese Asian Champions League winners Gamba Osaka, Ecuadorian champions Liga de Quito and Pacucha of Mexico. Something of a mid-season break!

In their 'semi-final' fixture against Gamba Osaka, United ran out 5-3 winners, with the far-flung local support in the 67,618 crowd treated to six goals in the final sixteen minutes of the game – a victory that earned them a place in the final against the champions of Ecuador.

Liga de Quito: Cevallos, N. Araujo, Calle, Campos, Calderon, Reasco, Urrutia, W. Araujo, Manso, Bolaños, Bieler. Substitutes: Ambrossi for Calle, Navia for Bolaños and Larrea for Reasco. Dominguez, Obregon, Delgado, E. Vaca, D. Vaca, Chango and Viteri not used.
United: Van der Sar, Rafael, Ferdinand, Vidic, Evra, Ronaldo, Carrick, Anderson, Park, Tevez, Rooney (1). Substitutes: Evans for Tevez, Neville for Rafael and Fletcher for Anderson. Kuszczak, Berbatov, Giggs, Nani, Scholes, Welbeck, O'Shea, Gibson and Amos not used.
Score: 1-0
Attendance: 68,862

Despite the atmosphere, not just for this deciding fixture, but for the previous ninety minutes against Osaka – being far removed from that of Old Trafford, with only the hardcore, travel-everywhere collection of United supporters doing their best to add some vocal encouragement to the proceedings – United did not disappoint.

Liga de Quito contributed little, although they did force Edwin van der Sar into making a couple of fine second-half saves from Manso and Araujo, when they suddenly decided that there was something at stake.

The twelve-hour journey from Manchester had taken its toll on some of the United players, but the Ecuadorians were certainly alert, with Bieler receiving a yellow card as early as the second minute for body-checking Ronaldo. A minute later, they were a little unfortunate not to take the lead, when the United defence was caught out by Bolaños who, instead of crossing, pushed the ball forward to an unmarked Manso, who missed a glaring opportunity from a few yards out.

United soon settled and both Tevez and Rooney had scoring opportunities, Cevallos alert to the danger, smothering the Argentinian's shot and pushing the latter's volley from the edge of the area wide.

Tevez had several other opportunities in the opening twenty minutes to give United the lead, but put one effort wide of the post and saw goalkeeper Cevallas make a fine save with another.

A Rooney effort, having beaten the offside trap, ended up on the roof of the net, then Carrick saw a 25-yard drive go narrowly wide, as United pumped up the pressure.

United's hopes of securing the trophy and title of World Champions took something of a dent three minutes into the second half, when Vidic was shown a straight red card for a retaliatory elbow to the face of Bieler, leaving United with only ten men.

The sending-off forced something of a reshuffle within the United ranks and Evans was sent on to supplement the defence, with the unfortunate Tevez, who had caused numerous problems for the opponents in the opening forty-five minutes, taken off.

The advantage of an extra man did little to bring the Liga de Quito side out of their shell and United, or indeed Wayne Rooney, continued to attack their defence with a vengeance, seeking to add to the two goals he scored in the previous game against Osaka.

But it wasn't until the seventy-second minute that he finally managed to get the better of Cevallos. A long through pass from Carrick picked out Ronaldo, hovering around the edge of the area. The ball was quickly played towards Rooney on the left, whose low drive across goal ended up in the bottom right-hand corner.

Ten minutes from time, a Rooney shot was blocked as it flew goalward and, as the minutes ticked away, van der Sar had to be alert to push a Bieler effort round the post, with his opposite number, Cevallos, having to rush out to the edge of his area to cut off the danger as Ronaldo closed in.

But there was to be no further scoring. United were crowned World Champions, Wayne Rooney was awarded a car from match sponsors Toyota for Man of the Tournament (beats a bottle of bubbly!) and another chapter in the club's long and glorious history was written.

Speaking after the 12,000-mile round trip, Sir Alex Ferguson said, 'It was terrific for the unity of the team. I think the players all enjoyed their time together. When you are at home in England you tend to go off in different directions after training.

'But when they're all away for a long spell like we've just been, they're together, they communicate very well and that's more important than anything. There was a fantastic atmosphere among the squad.'

40

Aston Villa (H)

5 April 2009

Successive defeats against Liverpool (4-2 at Old Trafford) and Fulham (2-0 at Craven Cottage) severely dented United's title hopes, with a red card for Wayne Rooney in the latter giving Sir Alex Ferguson selection problems for the forthcoming fixture against Aston Villa at Old Trafford.

With nine fixtures still to play, one more than second- and third-placed Liverpool and Chelsea, United held a one-point advantage over the Merseysiders and four over the Stamford Bridge club.

'We are going to kick on,' proclaimed the United manager. 'We are one point clear in the League and that is a great position to be in. We have had quite a time in terms of going to Japan, catching the leaders and then listening to all the nonsense about how good we are.'

United: Van der Sar, O'Shea, Neville, Evans, Evra, Ronaldo (2), Carrick, Fletcher, Nani, Giggs, Tevez. Substitutes: Macheda (1) for Nani and Welbeck for Tevez. Foster, Eckersley, Martin, Gibson and Park not used.
Aston Villa: Friedal, L. Young, Barry, A. Young, Milner, Carew (1), Agbonlahor (1), Davies, Petrov, Shorey, Cuellar. Substitutes: Reo-Coker for Milner. Guzan, Delfouneso, Knight, Salifou, Gardner and Albrighton not used.
Score: 3-2
Attendance: 75,409

Good they may well have been, but even good teams can be defeated and, at one point, it looked as though United's title hopes were slowly slipping away from them. It seemed that they were about to suffer their third consecutive Premier League defeat at the hands of Martin O'Neil's Aston Villa.

Prematch, Sir Alex Ferguson had problems. Wayne Rooney, Nemanja Vidic and Paul Scholes were all suspended, while Rio Ferdinand and Dimitar Berbatov were both out injured. Villa, equally, had not been without their problems, having recently suffered a humiliating 5-0 defeat at Liverpool.

Despite having five regulars out of action, United took the lead in the fourteenth minute through Cristiano Ronaldo, in what was to be one of his final games for the club prior to leaving for Real Madrid at the end of the campaign.

James Milner, for a reasons known only unto himself, passed the ball back to Brad Friedel, but placed it wide of the 'keeper, forcing him to handle the ball. Ryan Giggs then slipped the free-kick towards Ronaldo, and in a flash the ball was soaring into the top corner of the Villa net.

This should have been the springboard the current champions required to stamp their authority on the game, cementing their place at the top en route to yet another title. But it was not to be.

Recent injury victim Gary Neville returned to the side in a central defensive position, but it soon became arguable whether he would have been more vulnerable against the fleet-of-foot Ashley Young on the wing, or the more robust 6-foot 5-inch John Carew, with whom he came head to head.

On the half-hour, Neville struggled to contain Carew and the Villa front man had a free header from Barry's cross to beat van der Sar.

The United defence as a whole looked far from comfortable and it was looking as though the visitors would go on to impose themselves and further complicate United's title challenge.

Ferguson emerged from the dressing rooms after the interval and attempted to lift the Old Trafford crowd as he marched along the touchline.

But any vocal encouragement that vibrated from the stands was to little effect, as two minutes short of the hour mark they were two in front. Petrov robbed Ronaldo of the ball in the Villa half and released the ever threatening Carew. From his left-wing cross, missed by both Evra and Nani, Agbonlahor headed home at the far post.

Time wasn't exactly ticking out, but United, up until this point, did not look as though they were capable of salvaging anything from this game.

With ten minutes remaining, however, Ronaldo claimed his second of the afternoon with a low drive from outside the area.

Villa were now happy to slow the game down and hang on for the point they would be more than happy to return to the Midlands with. It was one eye on the action down on the pitch and the other on the scoreboard as the seconds and minutes ticked away.

With little to lose in the search for a winner, the United manager had thrown young Italian striker Frederico Macheda into the fray in the sixty-first minute for his League debut, not expecting any miracles, simply hoping that another forward on the pitch might create some sort of havoc in the Villa defence.

The seventeen-year-old former Lazio youth player had earned his place on the bench following a reserve-team hat-trick the previous Monday and, despite his inexperience at this level, he was quick to get involved.

But that elusive goal would not materialise and soon only seconds remained of the ninety minutes, with the assistant referee holding up his board and proclaiming that there would be a minimum of five minutes stoppage time.

We were in 'Fergie time'.

Few of those who were noted for leaving early had made their usual pre-full-time departure; they wanted to play their part in willing United to victory. That, however, looked beyond them, as indeed it looked beyond the players, as there were now only two of those five stoppage time minutes remaining.

As the young Italian attempted to push towards goal almost on the edge of the Villa penalty area, a Villa defender managed to toe poke the ball away, but only as far as Giggs, halfway inside the Villa half. Macheda continued to move into the Villa area and Giggs threaded the ball through.

Despite having his back to goal and a Villa defender behind him, Macheda flicked the ball with his right foot, turned quickly and curled the ball with his right past a helpless Friedal to snatch all three points for United.

The youngster wheeled away in delight, pursued by teammates, his celebrations earning him a booking from Mike Riley. It was a moment akin to Steve Bruce's winner against Sheffield Wednesday back in '93, a time when Macheda was only sixteen months old! It wasn't the goal that won United the title, but it gave them the momentum to go on and do so.

'You have to gamble,' said a relieved Sir Alex Ferguson. 'Winning is the name of the game at this club. We play the right way and we deserved to win because we tried to win the match.

'Yes, we take risks but risks are part of football. This club has been this way for a long, long time and I love the thrill of it myself.

'I love to see adventure.

'We took terrible risks and we didn't defend properly, but there is always a goal threat from us.

'There will always be a chance we will win the match and that is even more exciting than ever.'

41

Manchester City (H)

20 September 2009

It was the 152nd Mancunian derby, but as the days became hours and the hours became minutes, you could sense that this one was going to be slightly different from the majority of the others.

City had suddenly won the lottery. No longer did they have to shop at the local corner shop; they could now splash their cash wherever they wished – even get it delivered to their door.

Their manager, former United favourite Mark Hughes, had forgotten the one-time adoration from his time in the red shirt and was now more than happy to goad his former club and manager, telling anyone who wanted to listen that his City team were about to 'knock United off their perch' and that they would not be the dominant team in England for very much longer.

Hughes had spent £120 million during the summer: £24 million of that (rising to around £42 million) for a certain Carlos Tevez – another who was at one time the pin-up boy of the Stretford End, but since swapping his red shirt for light blue and having his image plastered over a city centre billboard, he became United enemy No. 1.

His old manager said, 'He was a good player for United, he did his job well. I have no complaints, though he says he didn't play enough football last year. I think he played plenty of football.'

'I'm not bothered about [the circumstances of Tevez's departure]. Believe me, I'm not the slightest bit worried. It happens and you can't keep all of the players, all of the time. I've always thought [South American] players were dominated by their agents. Their agents have a big say in their lives.'

United: Foster, O'Shea, Ferdinand, Vidic, Evra, Park, Anderson, Fletcher (2), Giggs, Berbatov, Rooney (1). Substitutes: Valencia for Park, Carrick for Anderson and Owen (1) for Berbatov. Kuszczak, G. Neville, Nani and Evans not used.
Manchester City: Given, Richards, Lescott, Touré, Bridge, Wright-Phillips, Barry (1), Dejong, Ireland, Bellamy (2), Tevez. Substitutes: Petrov for Dejong. Taylor, Zabaleta, Garrido, Weiss, Ball and Sylvinho not used.
Score: 4-3
Attendance: 75,066

Tevez had been a doubt for the highly charged derby due to an injury but, much to his new club's relief, he declared himself fit to play, as they were already without a £75-million strike force of Robinho Roque Santa Cruz and Adebayor – the latter suspended, the former injured. And it was Tevez who brought the game to life as early as the first minute, blocking a clearance by Foster, but to the relief of the home support, it was of little danger.

But that early scare ignited United, and within two minutes, they were in front.

Richards failed to pick up the overlapping Evra as he collected a throw-in and, from his cross, Rooney evaded two weak tackles before beating Given.

Giggs came close with a free-kick, and Berbatov fired the ball over, while at the opposite end Touré headed over, as the game bubbled into life with the United midfield just having the advantage.

The game, however, was suddenly turned on its head in the sixteenth minute when City equalised with what is best described as an absolute gift.

With the ball outside his area, Ben Foster attempted to dribble it into his box, as this would allow him to pick it up, but Tevez was quick to size up the situation and soon had Foster under pressure before robbing him of the ball, squaring it across the face of the goal to the waiting Barry, who side-footed the ball past a helpless Vidic on the goal line.

Attempting to get back into the game, Anderson shot wildly over the bar as United pressed forward, with the City defence looking distinctly nervous, although their central midfield advantage of three against two was beginning to tell.

Tevez was a constant danger but found his way into the referee's notebook for a rather clumsy challenge on Ferdinand. Then, with half-time beckoning, Touré intercepted a Rooney pass and played the ball forward. A dummied flick by Ireland found the Argentinian and with only Foster to beat, he hit the outside of the post from 8 yards out.

Two minutes into stoppage time, Lescott should perhaps have sent City in at the interval with a 2-1 advantage, but put the ball over from a good position in front of goal.

The second half was still in its infancy, with a mere five minutes gone, when United stunned the visitors by taking the lead. Evra, once again overlapping down the touchline, laid the ball back to Ryan Giggs, and his high cross was headed home by Darren Fletcher as he rose above Barry.

Park could have made it 3-1 in the fifty-first minute, but fired an Evra cross wide; it was a miss to be rued, as a minute later, City drew level once again. Bellamy, who was later to find himself face-to-face with an irate United supporter on the pitch, cutting inside from a Tevez pass let fly with an unstoppable shot into Foster's top right-hand corner. The United 'keeper was totally helpless.

Park once again shot wide, much to the frustration of the United support, but the red shirts were beginning to dominate.

Berbatov, 4 yards out and unmarked, was allowed a free header but was thwarted by Given, who made a fine save. The City 'keeper pulled off another from a Giggs volley as the Welshman connected with a Valencia cross.

Searching for the winner with only twelve minutes remaining, Sir Alex Ferguson threw Michael Owen into the fray in place of Berbatov, and within three minutes United were in front, although it was through Darren Fletcher, claiming his second of the game, who rose once again above the static City defence to head home a Giggs free-kick.

As the minutes ticked away, it looked as if United had done enough to secure all three points, but disaster struck in the final minute of normal time when Ferdinand tried a rather unnecessary pass back from more or less the halfway line and the ball was intercepted by Bellamy, who scurried off for goal before scooping the ball past Foster to level the scoring.

There was an audible click of seats in the home sections as disgruntled fans headed for the exits, but they should have known their team better by now, especially when the fourth official signalled four minutes of added time.

United pressed forward, hunting for the winner, as City tried to cling on to their point.

Winning a corner, Giggs sent it looping into the City area, but Given punched clear. The ball, however, fell to Rooney, but amid the panic and desperation he fired high over the top.

That was surely that, but moving into the fifth minute of stoppage time, much to the disgust of the visiting bench and support, a United free-kick was launched towards the City goal and was headed out as far as Giggs, who quickly threaded the ball in to Owen. The substitute slipped it past Given for a last-gasp winner.

The United manager down on the touchline leaped into the air, while Gary Neville took off down the touchline in the direction of the away support. Such is the joy of winning.

Mark Hughes was far from happy with the result and the manner in which it was achieved, blasting referee Martin Atkinson for adding on nearly seven minutes when the fourth official had signalled four.

Sir Alex Ferguson, on the other hand, was quick to remind his opposite number of his prematch comments and their hasty ambitions. 'For us it's unusual to accept that they're the top dogs in terms of media attention but sometimes you have got a noisy neighbour and have to live with it. What we can do, as we showed today, is you can get on with your life, put your television on and turn it up a bit louder.'

The United manager, however, blasted mistakes by Ben Foster and Rio Ferdinand that gifted two of the City goals, then bizarrely claimed United could have won 6-0.

'I am unhappy about the goals we conceded because it spoiled [what would have been] a really emphatic victory – we could have scored six or seven,' he said. 'We made horrendous mistakes which you don't associate with us and it kept them in the game.

'But that probably made it the best derby of all time so you're left wondering, what would you rather have had – won 6-0 or won the greatest derby? I would rather have won 6-0.'

42

Blackpool (A)
25 January 2011

A trip to the seaside in late January is certainly not something you would pencil into the diary, but following the postponement of the original fixture on 4 December due to a frozen pitch, twenty-four hours before kick-off, United's first League meeting on the Lancashire Riviera since a Second Division fixture in October 1974 was put back to a cold January evening with the nearby Pleasure Beach well and truly shut down for the winter and the famous illuminations having long disappeared from the promenade.

The Seasiders were finding it tough in the top flight; their last meeting with United at this level was way back in May 1971 and they had won only one of their last six fixtures, having lost the other five. United, on the other hand, were unbeaten in their previous half dozen, winning four and drawing two, but under Ian Holloway, the Bloomfield Road side were respected for their attacking play, despite their somewhat precarious position.

Blackpool: Kingson, Eardley, Cathcart (1), Evatt, Baptiste, Taylor-Fletcher, Vaughan, Adam, Grandin, Varney, Campbell (1). Substitutes: Harewood for Taylor-Fletcher and Phillips for Varney. Rachubka, Edwards, Southern, Sylvestre and Omerrod not used.
United: Van der Sar, Rafael, Smalling, Vidic, Evra, Nani, Gibson, Scholes, Fletcher, Rooney, Berbatov (2). Substitutes: Giggs for Gibson, Hernandez (1) for Rooney and Anderson for Rafael. Lindegaard, Owen, Fabio and Evans not used.
Score: 3-2
Attendance: 15,574

It was a roller-coaster ride for United a few hundred yards from the famous 'Golden Mile' at a Bloomfield Road, which had been completely redeveloped since the red hoards had last invaded the resort. On this occasion, they were certainly much better behaved, but all that is another story.

In a first-half performance when many of the travelling support, the United manager most likely included, would have considered walking down onto the promenade to see if there were any approaching trams that they could throw themselves in front of, the home side made a mockery of their League position and tore the visitors apart, taking a 2-0 lead. The United players looked like they had sampled some of the rides at the Pleasure Beach prior to kick-off.

As Mark Ogden wrote at the start of his match report for the *Daily Telegraph*, 'If they are looking for a new, white knuckle ride to tempt more visitors to Blackpool Pleasure Beach, they should call it the "Manchester United Experience" and issue a health warning that it is not for the fainthearted.' It was that bad.

Blackpool attacked the League leaders from the offset, not allowing them time on the ball, or the space to push forward from the back. Adam pinged passes around the pitch at ease as United stumbled around, unable to put any positive moves together, while missing the influential Ferdinand in defence.

They were also to find themselves behind after fifteen minutes, when former United youngster Craig Cathcart, a £500,000 signing following a successful loan spell, scored his first goal for the Tangerines.

Adam's corner floated into the United area, and Cathcart avoided the attention of Berbatov and headed home from 3 yards.

United struggled to get into the game as Blackpool continued to push forward at every opportunity. Vidic almost put through his own goal from another Adam cross, then Grandin should have increased the home side's lead, but shot wildly over.

Few of the United players could have been looking forward to the interval and the manager's presence in the dressing room, and their minds must have been lingering on such thoughts with only two minutes of the half remaining, when Adam swung over yet another corner, Gibson half-cleared off the line, and in stepped Campbell to head home.

Ferguson made his presence felt during that fifteen-minute break, replacing Gibson with Giggs for the second half. He was, however, to have little input on the proceedings, as Blackpool confidently held onto their lead.

A rash challenge by Rafael on Varney inside the 6-yard box brought immediate shouts for a penalty from the home support and players, but the referee waved away all their claims as Holloway almost threw a fit on the touchline.

An out-of-touch Rooney was replaced by Hernadez in the sixty-seventh minute as United continued to look for a way through the Blackpool defence and, unlike Giggs, the Mexican made an immediate impact, almost scoring within four minutes of coming on, his shot beating 'keeper Kingson, but it lacked any pace and was easily cleared by Cathcart.

The Blackpool defence was not so fortunate a minute later, when Darren Fletcher's low cross was volleyed home by Berbatov.

For the first time in the game, the home side looked fragile, as United realised that with eighteen minutes remaining they still had the opportunity to snatch a point.

It was only to take a further two minutes for the visitors to grab that equaliser, Hernandez evading the offside trap to latch onto a pass from Giggs before beating Kingson with a typical finish.

The United support, who had earlier contemplated what they had thought to be a wasted journey down the M55, really did like to be beside the seaside and they, like their tangerine-clad opposite numbers, sensed that a winner was now sure to follow.

And with only two minutes remaining, the turnaround was complete when Scholes found Berbatov, who left-footed the ball home.

'It is a result industry and we got a big result, which may have a big impact on the League at the end of the season,' exclaimed a somewhat relieved United manager at the end of the game.

'We have come from behind and that tells every one of those players in there what can be achieved by being at our best.

'We were deep in the mire in the first half, there is no question about that. We just couldn't handle Charlie Adam's free-kicks and corner kicks.

'The rhythm of our game was poor in the first half. Our penetration wasn't right.

'I just wonder if they (the United players) were overconfident before the game and they got a rude awakening. But once they got their finger out, we were a good team.'

43

Chelsea (H)

8 May 2011

His original game plan was to 'knock Liverpool off their ****ing perch'. A tongue-in-cheek comment perhaps, but one that stuck with him and certainly one that the United faithful could relate to, having suffered through years of Merseyside success, while their red-shirted heroes brought them only spasmodic FA Cup victories.

But the tide had certainly turned over the years. Slowly but surely, Liverpool's advantage in the number of League titles won had been whittled away and now there was a major concern at the opposite end of the East Lancs Road as the curator of the Old Trafford Museum was preparing a space for not simply the Premiership trophy, but the one that would mark Manchester United's nineteenth success, well and truly knocking the Anfield club off their perch – one that had been in a fragile condition for a number of years.

May had opened with a 1-0 defeat at the Emirates against Arsenal, followed by the 4-1 hammering of FC Shalke in the Champions League semi-final, giving United an aggregate 6-1 passage to a Wembley final against Barcelona. That, however, was put on the back-burner for now, as there were more pressing matters on the domestic scene, with Chelsea's visit to Old Trafford on the immediate horizon.

United led the Premier League by three points from their London rivals, with three games remaining, so victory was of the utmost importance. Losing at Highbury had been a blow, while Chelsea were on a run of five straight wins, ten games unbeaten, having clawed back twelve points from United. Included in all that was a 2-1 win over United at Stamford Bridge at the beginning of March.

A sixth straight victory for the Londoners would have put them right back in contention for the championship, while a victory for United would have seen that nineteenth title edge so much closer.

United: Van der Sar, Fabio, Ferdinand, Vidic (1), O'Shea, Valencia, Carrick, Giggs, Park, Rooney, Hernandez (1). Substitute: Evans for O'Shea and Smalling for Fabio. Kuszczak, Anderson, Berbatov, Nani and Scholes not used.
Chelsea: Cech, Ivanovic, Luiz, Terry, Cole, Lampard (1), Obi Mikel, Essien, Kalou, Drogba, Malouda. Substitutes: Alex for Luiz, Ramires for Obi Mikel and Torres for Kalou. Turnbull, Benayoun, Ferreira and Anelka not used.
Score: 2-1
Attendance: 75,445

Some of the supporters were still clicking through the Old Trafford turnstiles when a huge roar erupted from deeper inside the stadium. With the match having barely kicked off, surely it couldn't be a goal already, they thought, and they were relieved to see Chelsea kicking off as they made their way to their seats. The noise and the looks of jubilation on the faces of their fellow supporters, however, told them that they had indeed missed a goal.

From the kick-off, Giggs passed to Park, and the South Korean advanced towards the Chelsea goal. He slipped the ball forward, beyond the futile, misjudged attempted interception by Luiz. The pass found Hernandez and, with a dip of his shoulders, he wrong-footed Cech and right-footed the ball into the Chelsea net.

It was an ideal start, and one that clearly unsettled the visitors, their manager obviously unhappy on the touchline, venting his displeasure at a somewhat unconcerned Luiz. As the half progressed, the United players buzzed around the pitch, harassing the opposition at every opportunity, with Park enjoying arguably his best game in a red shirt, but it was Giggs who was running the show.

A 25-yard effort from Rooney was turned away by Cech and, from another accurate pass from the adventurous Park, Hernandez was only inches away from nudging the ball past the Chelsea 'keeper for a second time.

With the Chelsea defence totally disorganised, United scored a second in the twenty-third minute. The Giggs/Park duo once again created the opportunity with a short corner, the former getting past Kalou on the by-line before lifting the ball across goal, where Vidic moved in unchallenged to head home.

Van der Sar saved well from Kalou and Drogba, but the visitors were fortunate to remain at full strength when Ivanovic caught Rooney's heel. Already having been booked for a late tackle on Rooney, Howard Webb allowed the Chelsea player to stay on the pitch, when others would have undoubtedly have sent him off.

Chelsea manager Ancelotti later admitted that, if possible, he would have replaced ten of his players at half-time, but he kept it down to two. Another eight would more than likely have made little difference.

With a two-goal advantage, United were in the driving seat and happy to contain Chelsea, while continuing to pursue a third goal.

Eighteen minutes into the second half, United had strong claims for two penalties turned down, Howard Webb certainly not wishing to be drawn into any debate regarding handing United the title.

In the fifty-second minute, Valencia crossed from the right and the ball hit an outstretched Lampard arm, while eleven minutes later Valencia was brought down by John Terry. Despite the appeals from the United players and the equally voracious shouts from the crowd, Webb simply allowed play to continue.

Lampard pulled a goal back for Chelsea with twenty minutes remaining. Substitute Ramires crossed from the right, Ivanovic headed the ball down and Lampard touched the ball home.

Bringing on Torres was little more than desperation by the Chelsea manager as the game edged away from his team.

A goal-line clearance by Alex denied Rooney from getting his name on the scoresheet. The striker's inability to beat Cech with three other opportunities did likewise. Torres was equally as careless at the opposite end, bringing cries of 'you should have signed for a big club' echoing down from the stands.

With a minute remaining, Drogba lunged, high, late and two-footed, into Jonny Evans, but if Webb was not showing a red for previous Chelsea misdemeanours, he was not about to blot his copybook at this stage of the game. When he did blow his whistle to signal the end of the game, the delight of the United players was mirrored by the realisation of the Londoners that they had just been beaten by the champions elect.

After the game, Sir Alex Ferguson admitted that he would never have believed that his team were capable of overhauling Liverpool's eighteen League titles.

'Once we got that first title, the door opened and we improved and improved.

'We have still got to get that point at Blackburn and they are fighting relegation and so are Blackpool [United's final-day opponents]. But if you had said to me at the start of the season we'd need one point from our final home game, I'd have snapped your hand off. The players won't muck it up. They'll get the point.'

That vital point was secured in the 1-1 draw at Ewood Park, Blackburn, from a Wayne Rooney penalty, with a luckless Blackpool beaten 4-2 on the final day for good measure.

United were champions for a record nineteen times.

44

Arsenal (H)

28 August 2011

*Having defeated West Bromwich Albion 2-1 at the Hawthorns on the opening day of
the season and Tottenham Hotspur 3-0 at Old Trafford eight days later, it had been
the ideal start to 2011/12.*

*United can be a little slow out of the starting blocks, but this certainly was not one
of those seasons. United's next opponents, Arsenal, had not enjoyed the best of starts
and were languishing at the foot of the table along with Blackburn Rovers, West
Bromwich Albion and Tottenham Hotspur, having lost their opening two fixtures,
with manager Arsène Wenger coming in from some unwanted criticism.*

United: De Gea, Smalling, Jones, Evans, Evra, Nani (1), Cleverley, Anderson, Young
(2), Welbeck (1), Rooney (3). Substitutes: Hernandez for Welbeck, Park (1) for Nani
and Giggs for Anderson. Lindegaard, Ferdinand, Berbatov and Fabio not used.
Arsenal: Szczesny, Jenkinson, Djourou, Koscielny, Traoré, Ramsey, Coquelin, Walcott (1),
Rosicky, Arshavin, van Persie (1). Substitutes: Chamberline for Coquelin, Chamakh for
van Persie and Lansbury for Walcott. Fabianski, Miquel, Özyakup and Sunu not used.
Score: 8-2
Attendance: 75,448

If the Arsenal manager thought that some of the criticism aimed in his direction
following the opening two fixtures of the season was a little over the top, then
he must have been more than a little concerned as to what was about to come
his way on the return journey to London following the Sunday afternoon fixture
at Old Trafford. His plight was worsened by the under-the-microscope coverage
from Sky TV.

Both sides had absentees from their starting line-ups, but it had still taken United
twenty-two minutes to open the scoring. On the edge of the Arsenal area, Anderson
calmly lifted the ball over the heads of the Arsenal defence. Djourou allowed the ball
to bounce and in stepped Wellbeck to nod the ball past Szczesny.

Arsenal came close to drawing level five minutes later. Jonny Evans pulled down Theo
Walcott in a clumsy challenge, but Robin van Persie's penalty kick saw de Gea dive low
to his right to palm the ball away. Any hopes of an Arsenal fightback were over from
this point, the penalty save acting as an inspiration the rest of the United team.

It was a miss that was soon to be regretted, as United immediately swept upfield. Traoré failed to clear the ball with a weak header and it was snatched upon by Young, who, after side-stepping Coquelin, curled it past a helpless Szczesny.

De Gea confounded his critics with a superb double save from Arshavin and then van Persie, the former having been booked earlier for a terrible challenge on Jones. Not long afterwards, United lost Wellbeck to a hamstring injury, but this minor setback did little to their attacking options, throwing the goal menace of Hernandez into the fray.

A third United goal followed, four minutes before half-time. From the edge of the 18-yard box, Rooney tapped a free-kick to Young, who simply trapped the ball and stepped back, allowing Rooney to curl the ball wide of the once again helpless Arsenal 'keeper.

Arsenal pulled a goal back in stoppage time before the interval through Walcott, sneaking the ball between the legs of de Gea from a tight angle, but any hopes of a fightback were soon to evaporate into the Manchester autumn air.

Nineteen minutes into the second half, Rooney despatched another free-kick into the Arsenal net. Three minutes later, along with Smalling, he set up United's fifth for Nani, who chipped the ball over Szczesny.

Rooney was on fire, tormenting the Gunners at every opportunity, with another chip beating the harassed Arsenal 'keeper, but striking the post.

United scored their sixth in the seventieth minute, with Park, having come on as substitute, taking a pass from Young before sending a low left-footed shot into the far corner of the Arsenal net.

Arsenal were, by now, down and out, longing for the final whistle, which was still twenty minutes away, but they did manage to lessen the defeat somewhat with a second goal. Van Persie snatched a typical goal in the seventy-fourth minute.

But United, despite having taken their foot off the pedal a little, were far from finished. Jenkinson was sent off for bringing down Hernandez, having already been booked for a foul on Young, and Arshavin should also have gone for another reckless challenge on Young. Then, eight minutes from time, Walcott was penalised for a push on Evra inside the area and up stepped Rooney to claim his hat-trick from the penalty spot.

One minute into stoppage time, United completed the rout of a humiliated Arsenal side when Young scored his second of the afternoon with a looping right-footed shot from the edge of the area.

Members of the Arsenal board had missed those final two goals, deciding to leave early. Many of their support had wished they had missed the whole ninety minutes, such was United superiority over a club who they once considered as rivals.

'Shambolic' was one word used to describe the Londoners, but surprisingly, Sir Alex Ferguson felt sorry for them.

'You look at the Arsenal team and it was very weakened, but you still have to win these games. The criticism of Wenger is unfair. We live in a terrible, cynical world now and when you lose a few games, the judge is out and you see managers going early in the season many, many times over.

'We could have scored more goals,' he was to add, 'but you don't want to score more against a weakened team like that.'

From a supporter's point of view, you can never score too many goals, especially when goal difference could be crucial at the end of a season.

45

Manchester City (H)

23 October 2011

Backed by mega-rich Arab owners, Manchester City were now something of a force to be reckoned with. No longer could they be thought of as something of a laughing stock. They could, from time to time, still do something rather bizarre, but they were now serious title challengers – more so after having ended their thirty-five-year title drought with an FA Cup win in May 2011.

Thought of as 'noisy neighbours' by Sir Alex Ferguson, this latest 'derby' encounter, the 160th, was considered the biggest meeting between the two clubs for some forty years, if not the biggest of all time.

Prior to the Old Trafford encounter, City led the Premier League by two points, with both sides having played eight games. It was still early days, but victory for either side would give those championship aspirations the perfect boost.

Few of those making their way to the ground that Sunday lunchtime, or preparing to watch the game on television around the UK and abroad, had any inkling as to what they were about to witness.

United: De Gea, Smalling, Ferdinand, Evans, Evra, Nani, Fletcher (1), Anderson Young, Rooney, Welbeck. Substitutes: Hernandez for Nani and Jones for Anderson. Berbatov, Park, Fabio, Valencia and Lindegaard not used.
Manchester City: Hart, Richards, Kompany, Lescott, Clichy, Milner, Barry, Y. Touré, Silva, Agüero (1), Balotelli (2). Substitutes: Dzeko (3) for Balotelli, Nasri for Agüero and Kolarov for Milner. Pantilimon, Zabaleta, K. Touré and De Jong not used.
Score: 6-1
Attendance: 75,487

City had only won once at Old Trafford in thirty-seven years and the early chants from the United sections of 'Boring, boring City' were a little unfounded, as they had to date scored twenty-seven goals in their eight League outings. They added another to that total in the twenty-second minute, when Balotelli scored from what was really their first real attack on the United goal.

A Milner throw-in picked out Touré, who in turn found Silva, and his pass behind Smalling allowed Milner to pull the ball back to the feet of Balotelli, who calmly side-footed the ball past de Gea to give City the advantage.

Having scored, the Italian slowly turned around and lifted his shirt to reveal a T-shirt printed with the words 'Why always me?' and was promptly booked for his actions.

Prior to the goal, United had passed the ball about, but had failed to create any noteworthy scoring opportunities other than long-range efforts from Rooney, Nani and Young.

Only a goal behind at the interval, United had come back from much worse to win with a lot less than forty-five minutes remaining, so few of the red persuasion were really concerned. Within a minute of the restart, however, their confidence took something of a knock, as Jonny Evans was shown a straight red card for pulling back Balotelli on the edge of the United penalty area. Had he not done so, the City forward might well have scored, but even at 2-0 down, United would still have had eleven men.

But down to ten, they now had a fight on their hands against a City side who would gain much confidence from United's misfortune.

On the hour, Balotelli made it 2-0, beating de Gea from close range following a move between Richards, Silva and Milner. Nine minutes later, Agüero made it 3-0. That man Balotelli again flicked the ball to Milner, who released Richards into space and his cross into the 6-yard box, where United's defenders were too slow in reacting, Agüero beat Jones to score.

Without Vidic and with Ferdinand not enjoying the best of afternoons, the United defence was as strong as a wet cardboard box and were well and truly exploited by a rampant City.

It was a goal that shattered United's hopes of gleaning anything from the game and perhaps the worst possible thing to happen was for Darren Fletcher to pull a goal back ten minutes from time, curling home a side-footed effort from 25 yards.

Somewhat buoyed by the goal, the United players seemed to think that there was indeed the possibility of a fightback and threw caution to the wind.

But instead of coming close to yet another of those famed fightbacks, their forward assaults left holes at the back, holes that City were grateful to exploit, adding a further three goals in stoppage time.

City substitute Dzeko had already threatened on a couple of occasions and, when Ferdinand's attempted back pass went out for a corner in the ninetieth minute, Barry flicked the kick on, Lescott played the ball back and Dzeko could do nothing else but score: 4-1.

One minute into stoppage time, Dzeko sent a shot through Ferdinand's legs to notch the fifth. The United sections had been emptying well before the end, but there were now huge numbers of red empty seats around the stadium. Except, that is, in the Pozane-dancing City end. It had been a crazy final five minutes.

It was still not over, as Dzeko was to make it 6-1. Silva's first-time pass picked out the big forward to claim his hat-trick.

It had been eighty-one years since United conceded six goals at home in the League (United 4 Newcastle United 7, September 1930); fifty-six years since they lost at home by more than five (United 0 City 5, February 1955); fifty years since they conceded six at Old Trafford (United 2 Sheffield Wednesday 7, February 1961 FA Cup replay); forty-eight years since they lost 6-1 to anyone, anywhere (Burnley 6 United 1, December 1963); fifteen years since anyone scored six against them (Southampton 6 United 3, October 1996) and twelve years since they lost by five in any competition (Chelsea 5 United 0, October 1999). It was a black day in the history of Manchester United.

'I can't believe it, it is our worst day ever,' said a devastated United manager. 'It is the worst result in my history, ever. Even as a player I don't think I ever lost 6-1.

'I can't believe the scoreline. The first goal was a blow for sure but it was retrievable at 1-0.

'The sending-off was the killer. We kept attacking and it is all right playing to the history books, but common sense has to come in.

'The experience we have at the back, we should've realised and settled for that when it was 3-1 and 4-1.

'At 1-0 down with ten men we had two or three chances. We created good openings, but I think that encouraged us to keep going and our two full backs were playing like wingers.

'At times it was two versus three at the back and that was suicidal, crazy.'

46

Manchester City (A)

9 December 2012

It had been a long summer for Manchester United supporters, much longer than normal, and if you ventured out around Manchester city centre then it was made much worse by the sight of more light-blue shirts than usual.

United had been 2011/12 champions for long enough to make a cup of tea on that final afternoon of the season, but there was a surreal silence around the Stadium of Light, as City were still playing and only drawing against Queens Park Rangers. But with the Londoners learning via the Etihad scoreboard that they were safe from relegation, they allowed their concentration to drift and began thinking of a relaxing couple of weeks on the beach. City snatched a dramatic winner and the title suddenly swung across Manchester.

There was, of course, only one way to recover from the disappointment of seeing the championship slip away so cruelly, one way to gain revenge, and that was to go out and reclaim the title. Snatch it back from the hands of those 'noisy neighbours'.

It was to be a season of immense drama, a roller-coaster ride like never before and one where any number of fixtures could have found their way into the pages of this book.

Manchester City: Hart, Zabaleta (1), Kompany, Natasic, Clichy, Silva, Y. Touré (1), Barry, Nasri, Agüero, Balotelli. Substitutes: K. Touré for Kompany, Tevez for Balotelli and Dzeko for Y. Touré. Pantilimon, Lescott, Maicon and Garcia not used.
United: De Gea, Rafael, Ferdinand, Evans, Evra, Valencia, Carrick, Cleverley, Young, Rooney (2), van Persie (1), Substitutes: Smalling for Evans, Jones for Valencia and Welbeck for Cleverley. Johnstone, Giggs, Hernandez and Scholes not used.
Score: 3-2
Attendance: 47,136

It was tight at the top of the Barclays Premier League prior to one of the most important Manchester 'derby' fixtures of recent times. It was also red at the top, with United holding a three-point advantage over their local rivals, both having played the same number of games. Yes, it was only halfway through the campaign, but a victory to United would open up a six-point gap – not uncatchable, certainly not with United's kamikaze streak, but a decent advantage to hold.

Victory for City, on the other hand, would pull them level, and give them renewed hope and confidence to approach the remainder of the season with a skip in their step, knowing that the opportunity was there to retain the title that they had waited so long to get their hands on.

It would be 'one of United's best-ever results if they were to win' confessed the United manager, as much a gee-up to his squad as anything else.

'We are determined to make up for losing the title to them last season,' he went on. 'The way we lost it made it even harder to accept. This season we are determined to win the title back.

'I will never forget how I felt that night after we had lost it and that will give us more motivation, definitely.'

Ferguson took something of a cautious approach with a 4-4-1-1 line-up, with Wayne Rooney dropping back behind van Persie, but it was one that offered more attacking options than the team selection in last season's corresponding fixture.

The game sprang into life from the first whistle, giving the rival supporters a taste of what was to come. Carrick fouled Agüero, and then Rooney sent Silva sprawling before catching Touré. Ferdinand upended Agüero to the delight of the away support.

But the opening minutes belonged to City, with the unpredictable Balotelli to the fore, and a free-kick being pushed behind by de Gea and then squandering a Clichy cutback.

United, however, were more than content to simply soak up the pressure and wait patiently for the opportunity to break forward. With sixteen minutes gone, that opportunity arose. Ashley Young headed Evra's pass over the head of Zabaleta towards van Persie, the winger continuing his run to pick up the return ball. With the City full-back out of position, Young accelerated forward before passing the ball inside to Rooney, whose half-hit effort left Joe Hart stranded as it headed for the far corner. Ten touches was all it took for the visitors to score.

City lost their defensive mainstay and captain Vincent Kompany to an injury five minutes later and they were to go further behind in the twenty-ninth minute, with their defence once again caught flat-footed.

Rafael, never needing any excuse to get forward, ran onto a pass from Valencia and his cross slipped through the legs of Clichy before landing at the feet of Rooney, who swept the ball past Hart to put United 2-0 in front. It was his 150th goal for the club.

Five minutes after the break, Mancini removed Balotelli from the action, sending on the more alert Tevez, hoping he could prove to be a thorn in the side of this former club.

His influence should have mattered little when, on the hour, Young beat Hart, pouncing on the ball after a van Persie shot had rebounded off the woodwork. His joy and that of the United support immediately in front of him was soon dampened as a linesman judged him to be in an offside position, a decision that was later proved to be wrong.

It came as a relief to City and stirred them into action, pulling a crucial goal back within a minute.

De Gea made a superb double stop from Tevez and Silva, but the former managed somehow to direct the ball toward Yaya Touré, who hit the ball low past the United 'keeper.

City were back in the game.

Evra had a penalty claim disallowed, after being caught by Kolo Touré, while missing a Rooney corner in front of goal. Van Persie headed wide from a Cleverley cross and then, at the opposite end, Silva almost equalised, causing havoc in the United area, but could only watch in anguish as his shot hit de Gea on the shoulder and rebounded off the bar.

With only four minutes remaining, City kept their championship hopes alive. The United defence failed to clear a Tevez corner kick and Zabaleta drove the ball home from the edge of the area.

Credit was due to the home side for their fightback, but United should not have found themselves in this position and certainly would not have been had the linesman got things right.

The game was heading into stoppage time when Tevez gave away a free-kick with a foul on Rafael some 25 yards out. Van Persie stood over the ball as City organised their defensive wall, which Tevez left to cover Rooney. The Dutchman curled the ball towards goal and it took a deflection off Nasri's right leg before looping over a helpless Hart.

Ferdinand was hit just above the eye with a coin amid the celebrations, the United defender also coming in for close attention from a pitch-encroaching City supporter.

But it was all over. United had snatched yet another victory right at the death and another that would prove to be of vital importance.

Celebrating the victory, Sir Alex Ferguson said, 'Today was a special one simply because City haven't lost at home for two years and both of us are contending at the top of the League.

'It's a great day for us, to get six points clear and beat our closest rivals, especially with what happened last season. We've waited a long time for this to happen and I'm sure it means everything to everyone at the club and all the fans.

'You could not take your eyes off it. It was such an engrossing game. We had a goal that was perfectly onside ruled out, and they go up the pitch and score.

'That's the kind of game football is – it can kill you and kick you in the teeth.

'They deserved to come back when it was 2-2, but up to that point, I thought we were far better than them.

'They've had a great home record and to spoil that is a great feeling.

'It was crazy but it's been like that all season.'

47

Newcastle United (H)

26 December 2012

Peace and goodwill to all men is the Christmas message, especially if you reside in the North East of England. It might only extend to a twenty-four-hour period, but that is better than nothing.

Boxing Day had seen Manchester City journey to the one-time hotbed for soccer talent to face Sunderland, hoping to claw back a few points as they pursued United at the top of the table, desperate to hold onto the trophy that they had secured back in May. But they became unstuck, losing 1-0 to what was considered an ordinary Sunderland side.

United, on the other hand, entertained Newcastle United at Old Trafford, the Geordies having lost four of their last five games, while the hosts had lost only one and drawn one of their previous half-dozen, so another victory would do much more than simply consolidate their position at the top of the pile.

United: De Gea, Smalling, Ferdinand, Evans (1 plus 1 own goal), Evra (1), Valencia, Carrick, Scholes, Giggs, van Persie (1), Hernandez (1). Substitutes: Cleverley for Scholes and Fletcher for Hernandez. Lindegaard, Vidic, Buttner, Wooton and Tunicliffe not used.
Newcastle United: Krul, Simpson, Coloccini, Santon, Williamson, Perch (1), Anita, Bigrimana, Marveaux, Cisse (1), Ba. Substitutes: Obertan for Bigrimana and Ameobi for Ba. Elliot, Ferguson, Tavernier and Campbell not used.
Score: 4-3
Attendance: 75,596

Despite Newcastle United's recent form, United could certainly not take things for granted and there was no Christmas cheer from the visitors, while United, in the opening forty-five minutes at least, looked as though they were suffering from something of a festive hangover.

Newcastle began with the forward threat of Demba Ba up front on his own, while attempting to barricade the midfield and United's route to goal, and they looked something of threat from early on, going a goal in front after only four minutes.

Hernandez attempted a crossfield pass to Evans, but somehow Carrick got in the way and attempted to control the somewhat powerful ball. Unable to do so, it allowed Newcastle to break and de Gea could only block Demba Ba's shot, the ball skidding conveniently off the wet surface to the feet of Perch, who slipped the ball home to give the visitors the lead. It was a goal that was very similar to the one conceded at Swansea in the previous match.

It took United until the twenty-fifth minute to draw level, when a van Persie free-kick on the right fell to Smalling and then Hernandez, who took one touch before blasting a shot towards the Newcastle goal. Krul blocked the ball with his foot, Jonny Evans reacting the quickest, getting in front of Danny Simpson to put United level from 5 yards out.

But amid a post-Christmas hangover, instead of taking a grip of the game, there was some poor defensive play, with Ferdinand unusually out of sorts. Alongside him Evans, despite having scored, did not look too happy. In midfield, Carrick, Scholes and Giggs also struggled against the greater numbers of Newcastle central line. Up front, Hernandez struggled manfully, but was often dispossessed near goal.

Three minutes after putting United level, Jonny Evans scored his second of the night. Unfortunately, on this occasion it was at the wrong end. Simpson crossed and Evans diverted the ball past de Gea, but the United defender looked as though he had been spared the blushes by a linesman's flag, signalling that Cisse was in an offside position.

Referee Mike Dean, however, following a brief conversation, overruled his assistant and the goal stood, much to the annoyance of the United manager.

His annoyance was to continue as the teams came out for the second half, with Ferguson continuing to debate the events of the twenty-eighth minute with the match official. Mike Dean was later to say that, due to it being an own goal, it did not matter that a Newcastle player was in an offside position.

Prior to the interval, United were fortunate not to go further behind, as Hernandez, having taking on the role of an extra defender, tripped Marveaux just outside the penalty area and, from the free-kick, the same player could only watch in anguish as his effort hit the bar.

The manager's touchline actions galvanised the crowd for the second forty-five minutes and, thirteen minutes after the restart, United were level. Perch headed the ball clear following a United attack, but only as far as Evra, who struck a low shot past Krul from outside the area as Ba made a half-hearted challenge.

Many expected United to now step up a gear and go on to victory, but once again the game spun on its head.

Former United old-boy Gabriel Obertan came on as substitute for Newcastle and almost immediately was involved in the sixty-eighth-minute goal that once again saw the visitors take the lead. Having moved past Smalling, his cut-backed pass was taken first time by Cisse to beat de Gea with a firm left-footed shot.

But yet again, United drew level.

Three minutes later, Krul managed to block a van Persie effort, but the Dutchman made no mistake at the second time of asking.

With the game moving into overdrive, Hernandez headed against the post while also rounding Krul but was unable to finish things off. Van Persie was also to shoot wide. Then, as play swung back and forth, Sammy Ameobi also hit the post at the opposite end with five minutes remaining, after cutting in from the right, with the ball rebounding to a thankful de Gea.

Time, however, was running out, and as the clock showed ninety minutes had been played, Carrick once again opened up the Newcastle defence, crossing into a packed penalty area, with Hernandez sliding in to make it 4-3 to United, with no time for a Newcastle fightback.

United were, however, fortunate to finish the game with eleven men, as Valencia, already booked, caught Anita with a poorly timed tackle, but was let off by the referee, perhaps not wishing to deal with the wrath of the United manager for a second time in one night. He did have to deal with irate Newcastle players and officials as he left the field at the end.

This was the eighth game this season that United had fought back from behind to win the game – their refusal to give up was indeed the mark of champions!

'Absolutely brilliant they were,' enthused the United manager. 'I wish it was the last game of the season. It tells you about the courage of our team. It was fantastic. We never gave in. We made a host of chances in the second half. We improved our game enormously, which we had to do.

'We had a lot of bad decisions against us in the first half. That could have demoralised the team. But they didn't give in. That is the great quality they have. I am pleased. We were down three times and came back three times, then scored the winner.

'It is a really significant result for us. It puts us in a good position. But as I always say about December, it is a month that tells you everything.'

48

Aston Villa (H)

22 April 2013

Spring was in the air and things were beginning to get a bit hotter.

On Sunday 21 April, United held a thirteen-point lead at the top of the Barclays Premier League, but had played two games more than their across-city neighbours.

City travelled to London to face an in-form but sometimes erratic Tottenham. United were due to face Aston Villa at Old Trafford the following evening. The Midlands side had spent most of the season fighting off the threat of relegation.

By Sunday teatime, United were still thirteen points clear, having played one game more as well as enjoying a massive goal difference, as City's hopes of retaining the title took a bit more than a severe bashing at White Hart Lane, returning despondently north on the end of a 3-1 defeat.

Victory against Aston Villa would ensure United of the title. Not only that, victory in their final five games would also give them ninety-six points, setting a new record, passing Chelsea's ninety-five in season 2005.

But first they had to achieve victory under the Old Trafford floodlights.

United: De Gea, Rafael, Jones, Evans, Evra, Valencia, Carrick, Giggs, Kagawa, Rooney, van Persie (3). Substitutes: Welbeck for Rooney. Lindegaard, Ferdinand, Hernandez, Nani, Cleverley and Buttner not used.
Aston Villa: Guzan, Lowton, Baker, Vlaar, Bennett, Weimann, Delph, Agbonlahor, Westwood, N'Zogbia, Benteke. Substitutes: El Ahmadi, for N'Zogbia and Clark for Bennett. Given, Bent, Holman, Sylla and Bowery not used.
Score: 3-0
Attendance: 75,591

Villa had threatened not to lie down to the prospective champions, using their recent revival as proof that they were capable of causing an upset and keeping the title race open for a while yet, but they were to find themselves a goal behind after only two minutes, the cry of 'Champions' echoing around the ground much sooner than had been anticipated.

Rooney's sublime pass picked out Valencia on the right and, after wrong-footing Bennett, he cut the ball back for Rafael. The young Brazilian's cross found and Giggs, who turned the ball across goal to the feet of van Persie, who side-footed home from close range.

The party had begun.

The goal invigorated both the players and the crowd and United chased a quick second, with Rafael hitting the post.

Villa attempted something of a fightback, Weimann sending Benteke through on goal, but the Villa front man shot over the advancing de Gea.

Rooney looked to be enjoying his temporary midfield role, as well as the space that was afforded him, and in the thirteenth minute produced a forward pass of immense accuracy from inside his own half, picking out van Persie moving forward towards the edge of the Villa penalty area. As the ball dropped from the night sky, the Dutchman never altered his stride and caught the ball on the volley, blasting it past a helpless Guzan to put United two up with one hand firmly on the championship trophy.

It was a goal that must go down as one of the best ever scored at the famous old ground.

Twelve minutes before the break, the red-and-white ribbons were secured to the Premier League trophy when Kagawa picked out Giggs, sneaking behind the Villa defence, the Welshman passing to van Persie, who side-stepped Guzan in the Villa goal before shooting past Vlaar on the line.

Villa, to their credit, never gave up and Weimann had an effort cleared off the line by van Persie, Ferguson's preseason signing making the real difference between being champions and runners-up.

Some sloppy defending almost allowed Benteke to pull a goal back, but de Gea saved well. The United 'keeper was also called upon to tip an El Ahmadi effort over the bar.

Rooney put a shot over the bar, while Kagawa should have done much better in the seventy-seventh minute with one effort that ended high in the Stretford End.

The game was played out amid a chorus of terrace anthems and, as the final whistle blew, the delight on the United players' faces – none more so than van Persie's – told you how much winning, or indeed regaining the title from Manchester City, meant to them.

Thousands of camera flashes lit up the stands as the crowd saluted their heroes. Who would have thought that, having waited twenty-six years between championships, we would see thirteen during the reign of Sir Alex Ferguson?

On his thirteenth success, the United manager said, 'If you are going to manage this club, you have to accept there is a sacrifice you have to make.

'You need to make a commitment to it. There is also an expectation to live up to.

'You really need to win all the time. It is the only way you can fulfil the expectation and avoid the criticism.'

He added, 'The hardest thing is to maintain a level of success that keeps going year after year. There might be several factors involved in it. I have never looked back, always forward. And we've had continuity of management, not just myself but my staff. That helps.

'I am delighted that we are sitting here (champions with four fixtures remaining). I would take that any time.

'But, of course, I am surprised. With the competition we have in the Premier League we expect it to be tough. It is tough. The competition is more severe now.

'That is why we are delighted with what we have achieved.'

49

Swansea City (H)

12 May 2013

On the night of 7 May, the social media websites, along with Sky Sports, went into overdrive with the story that Sir Alex Ferguson was about to retire at the end of the current season. The rumour had begun at a club golf day and was about to be both back- and front-page news in the following morning's newspapers.

It was also soon proved to be more than a rumour, with a club statement confirming that the United manager was indeed about to walk away from the club, and the stadium, that he had built following his arrival from Aberdeen, way back in November 1986.

The 2012/13 Premiership title, United's twentieth, had of course been added to the long list of honours under the man from Govan, with the trophy due to be presented at the final home game of the season against Swansea City. It was a presentation that was now going to take a back seat. Amid the celebrations, there was going to be sadness. Tears would be shed, even by those hardened members of the Red Army, as they said their farewells to man who had brought them more memorable moments than they could ever have hoped for.

Tickets had already been scarce on the ground, some reportedly changing hands for £1,000, but with the game now billed as Sir Alex Ferguson's farewell, they were approaching silly prices. Everyone wanted to say 'I was there'.

United: De Gea, Jones, Vidic, Ferdinand (1), Evra, Kagawa, Scholes, Carrick, Welbeck, Hernadez (1), van Persie. Substitutes: Valencia for Scholes, Anderson for Welbeck and Giggs for Hernadez. Lindegaard, Buttner, Evans and Cleverley not used. Swansea: Tremmel, Taylor, Chico, Williams, Tiendalli, Dyer, Routledge, Britton, De Guzman Hernadez, Michu (1). Substitutes: B. Davies for Taylor, Augustien for Hernadez and Rangel for Michu. Cornell, Monk, Lamah and Shechter not used.
Score: 2-1
Attendance: 75,572

He had strolled out of the old players' tunnel, the only part of the original Old Trafford still in existence, on the afternoon of Saturday 22 November 1986 to salute the 42,235 present for his first home match as Manchester United manager against Queens Park Rangers. His record as manager of Aberdeen had preceded him, but no one knew what a momentous roller-coaster ride they were about to endure at the hands of the man from Govan. Now, almost twenty-seven years down the line, some of those same supporters were among the 75,572 present to say farewell to arguably the greatest football manager of all time and celebrate Manchester United's record-breaking twentieth title.

There was certainly no fanfare of trumpets to herald his arrival, but on that final afternoon, 'My Way' and 'The Impossible Dream' were blasted out over the PA system as a guard of honour lined up at the mouth of the tunnel to salute the man of the moment.

Old Trafford was a mass of red and white. Every seat had a flag – even the Swansea supporters were given white ones celebrating the club's Capital One Cup success. These were complimented with dozens of home-made efforts, all adding to the occasion.

The ninety minutes of football were always going to be overshadowed by the outgoing manager, but there was also another farewell to be said, as Paul Scholes had also announced his retirement, albeit for the second time, hoping to mark his 717th appearance with his 156th goal for the club.

Wayne Rooney was a surprise omission from the United squad, but it was to make little difference to the outcome of the game, which was played out against a backdrop of rain. United almost took the lead within five minutes of the start, Hernandez hitting the underside of the Swansea crossbar. Scholes stumbled in an attempt to shoot, while another Hernadez attempt went over.

Flores deflected yet another Hernadez effort wide and Tremmel in the Swansea goal had little trouble dealing with poorly hit shots from Evra and Scholes.

Kagawa was denied a penalty when brought down by Taylor as United continued to push forward, but a goal would not materialise.

It was not, however, until the thirty-ninth minute that United finally managed to break the deadlock. A Robin van Persie free-kick struck Williams and it was enough of an opportunity for Hernadez to pounce on, firing home from close range.

Van Persie could have increased that advantage before the break, but Tremmel did well to save a powerful drive; the Dutchman should perhaps have passed to Scholes, who was better placed, instead of shooting, his effort going high and wide.

Four minutes into the second half, Swansea drew level through Michu, flicking the ball past de Gea with the outside of his foot after Jones had attempted to head clear a Dyer's cross.

'You're getting sacked in the morning' the Swansea support taunted Ferguson and they almost had even more to shout about when Routledge escaped the clutches of Ferdinand before shooting narrowly wide.

Scholes made his Old Trafford exit in the sixty-sixth minute to a standing ovation, departing a stage upon which he stood shoulder to shoulder with United's greatest names, unable to deliver that farewell goal, despite cries of 'shoot' whenever he received the ball. The trademark passes were all there. Only the goal was missing.

Swansea tried their best to spoil the party and, as the minutes ticked away, it looked as though the Old Trafford curtain was going to come down on Sir Alex Ferguson's career in football with a draw. But this was Manchester United, Ferguson's Manchester

United, a team that never gave up and, of course, there would surely be some 'Fergie time' added on at the end.

Indeed there was, but United did not need it on this occasion to claim victory, as with three minutes remaining, a van Persie corner found its way to the opposite side of the Swansea penalty area and a waiting Rio Ferdinand, unmarked, blasted the ball home for his first goal in more than five years: United's twentieth goalscorer in their twentieth championship-winning campaign.

There was only a modest three minutes of 'Fergie time' before the final whistle blew and a sadness enveloped Old Trafford.

Suddenly, the manager was alone in the centre circle, microphone in hand. 'My retirement doesn't mean the end of my life with the club. I'll be able to now enjoy watching them rather than suffer with them,' he announced. 'But if you think about it ... those last-minute goals, the comebacks, even the defeats are all part of this great football club of ours.

'When I had bad times here, the club stood by me. All my staff stood by me, you stood by me, and your job is now to stand by our new manager. That's important.

'To all of you – you have been the most fantastic experience of my life. I've been very fortunate. I have been able to manage some of the greatest players in the country.

'It's also important to go out as a winner. That's really important at this club. It's all I ever wanted to do here – be a winner.'

A few more words and he was gone, but only until the stage was set for the presentation of the championship trophy.

Sir Alex's two former captains, Steve Bruce and Bryan Robson, carried the trophy onto the pitch and, one by one, the players were presented with their medals. A lap of honour followed, the manager accompanied by his eleven grandchildren, all ready to enjoy more of their grandfather's company.

50

West Bromwich Albion (A)

19 May 2013

Having been in charge of Manchester United for 1,499 competitive fixtures, there were still ninety more minutes, plus, of course, 'Fergie time', to play before the guv'nor from Govan could walk away from the day-to-day management of the club that he had built into one of the top three in the world and arguably the best supported in the world.

One final hurrah, one final wave to the travelling Red Army, then it was over, a historic career confined to the history books and a career that will surely never be matched or surpassed.

West Bromwich Albion: Foster, Olsson (1 own goal), Ridgewell, McAuley, Jones, Yacob, Morrison (1), Brunt, Dorrans, Mulumbu (1), Long. Substitutes: Lukaku (3) for Ridgewell, Fortune for Morrison and Rosenberg for Long. Myhill, Popov, Dawson and Tamas not used.
United: Lindegaard, Valencia, Evans, Jones, Buttner (1), Anderson, Carrick, Cleverley, Kagawa (1), van Persie (1), Hernandez (1). Substitutes: Giggs for Cleverley, Scholes for Kagawa and Ferdinand for Evans. De Gea, Evra, Vidic and Januzaj not used.
Score: 5-5
Attendance: 26,438

Like the Swansea City match the previous weekend, the final fixture of the season was always going to be more than ninety minutes of football. It was not simply bringing the curtain down on a campaign that had seen Manchester United once again crowned Premier League champions, it was Sir Alex Ferguson's final fixture as manager of the club and the atmosphere conjured up by the travelling support would ensure, no matter the score, that it would be a day to remember.

As the afternoon unfolded, it was something that could never have been stage managed and was indeed a fitting finale.

With nothing to play for, the game could easily have been played out at a pace normally reserved for testimonials and friendlies, but the players, certainly those in red shirts, wanted to say their farewells to 'the Boss' with a victory, and one achieved the Manchester United way. West Bromwich Albion were not simply there to make up the numbers, to be the supporting cast, to make a few extra pounds by adding a thirty-eight-page supplement to their programme as a tribute to the opposition manager, throwing in a guard of honour before kick-off for good measure, but as the game progressed it certainly began to look that way.

Shinji Kagawa headed United into the lead in the sixth minute, van Persie interchanging passes with Cleverley before bringing Buttner into the action. The deputy full-back found Hernandez with a 40-yard pass, with the ball swung over to Kagawa who headed home from inside the 6-yard box.

A Valencia cross from the right took a deflection off Jonas Olsson to beat former United 'keeper Ben Foster for United's second two minutes later.

Hernadnez should have made it three, but sent his header wide of the target. Then, on the half-hour, it was 3-0, full-back Buttner finding himself in the Albion area to fire a low shot into the far corner, as the game took on a completely one-sided look.

Prior to the interval, Morrison pulled a goal back for the home side after Buttner lost possession, but it was looked upon as nothing more than a consolation effort, even with forty-five minutes remaining.

Foster pulled off an excellent save immediately after the restart, blocking a Hernandez effort, showing superb reflexes to make a second equally good save as the ball cannoned off McAuley.

But suddenly the game changed course as second-half substitute Lukaku scored a second for West Brom and the game suddenly took on a completely new outlook.

Van Persie restored United's two-goal advantage from Valencia's cross in the fifty-third minute, with Hernandez adding a fifth when he tapped in a Giggs cross ten minutes later after the Welshman had been released down the left by Kagawa.

Olsson could have won an award for the miss of the season when he fired the ball over from underneath the bar, then at the opposite end Buttner hit the bar and a Giggs effort landed on top of the netting.

Scholes was then given his final appearance in a red shirt and, although the script did not allow for a farewell goal, it did deliver a yellow card for the familiar, clumsy, late challenge.

Lukaku made it 5-3 with ten minutes remaining, then Mulumbu scored a fourth for the Albion, bundling the ball past a defender, sending the home fans into a frenzy.

With four minutes remaining, a hesitant United defence allowed Lukaku to complete his hat-trick and put West Brom level.

Never before had a Premier League match finished 5-5, but would United score a sixth in 'Fergie time'?

Few would have complained had the game gone on until darkness fell, but a couple of minutes over the ninety, referee Mike Oliver brought an end to the game, a season and a career – two careers if you include Paul Scholes.

A quick shake of the hand with Albion manager Steve Clarke, and Sir Alex Ferguson marched onto the pitch to embrace his players before heading to the end that housed the majority of the travelling support.

With his hands held above his head, he saluted the United support then, prompted by his senior players, Ryan Giggs and Rio Ferdinand, he walked forward alone and bowed to the multitude behind the goal.

The home-made banners were again out in force. 'For twenty-six years you gave us the world' said one. 'Thanks for all the memories' said another.

Having accepted the applause of the supporters and his players, he turned and made his way to the tunnel, eventually disappearing from view.

Gone, but certainly not forgotten.

For once, Sir Alex Ferguson refused to give interviews after the game, uttering only three words for the men of the world's press to work on: 'Emotional, very emotional.'

It was left to West Bromwich Albion's manager, Steve Clarke, to help fill out the column inches, with the fellow Scot saying after the customary glass of red wine, 'I think he's just ready for his retirement to be honest.

'He said it was a good game, he complimented us on the way we played. For Sir Alex, it's a great occasion, it's a great finale.

'I'm not sure Sir Alex would say it was a fitting way to end. He told me it's the first time that any team he's been involved with has given away a three-goal lead and they did it twice in one game [they had actually done it before]. That's something for us to savour.

'It's great that he has gone out as a champion. He deserves to enjoy his retirement.'

Sources & Acknowledgements

Newspapers Used in Research

Manchester Evening News, Daily Mirror, Sunday Mirror, People, Daily Express, Sunday Express, Times, Sunday Times, Guardian, Observer, Daily Telegraph, Sunday Telegraph, The Sun, Star, Daily Mail, Mail on Sunday, Independent, Sunday Independent, Today, Galloway Gazette, Galloway Advertiser and Wigtonshire Free Press, Sunday Post, Sunday Mail, Evening Times, Glasgow Herald.

Acknowledgements

Kenny Ramsey (cover photograph and image 28 in the picture section), Kevin Donald and Andrew Dobney.

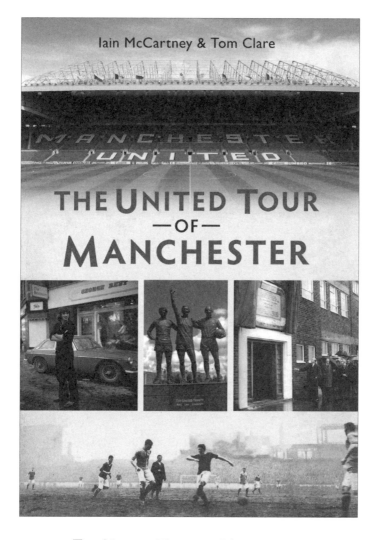

THE UNITED TOUR OF MANCHESTER

Iain McCartney & Tom Clare

Ever wondered what the connection between Manchester United and Bramhall Hall is? Do you know the exact location where the Professional Footballers Association was founded? Where does the first captain of Manchester United to lift a major trophy lie at rest? The answers are to be found in this book, which takes you on the United Tour of Manchester.

978 1 4456 1913 2
128 pages, full colour

Available from all good bookshops or order direct
from our website www.amberleybooks.com

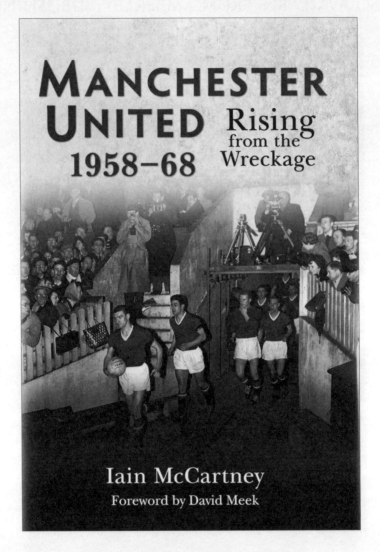

MANCHESTER UNITED 1958–68
RISING FROM THE WRECKAGE

Iain McCartney

'A remarkable feat of research and hugely admirable'
WHEN SATURDAY COMES

Rising from the Wreckage is the definitive story of Manchester
United's resurgence, from the ashes of a German runway to a balmy
May evening at Wembley and the pinnacle of European football.

978 1 4456 1798 5
352 pages, including 55 images

Available from all good bookshops or order direct
from our website www.amberleybooks.com